ELO

A VISUAL BIOGRAPHY

LAURA SHENTON

ELO

A VISUAL BIOGRAPHY

LAURA SHENTON

WP
WYMER
PUBLISHING
Bedford, England

First published in Great Britain in 2024
by Wymer Publishing
www.wymerpublishing.co.uk
Tel: 01234 326691
Wymer Publishing is a trading name of Wymer (UK) Ltd

ISBN: 978-1-918419-00-9

Edited by Jerry Bloom

Typeset and Design by Andy Bishop/Tusseheia Creative
Printed and bound by Halstan, Amersham, Buckinghamshire.

Cover photos © Alan Perry Concert Photography

A catalogue record for this book is available from the British Library.

Except where noted, all photos are from the archives of
Alan Perry Concert Photography.

Special thanks to Martin Hutchinson for his valuable contribution.

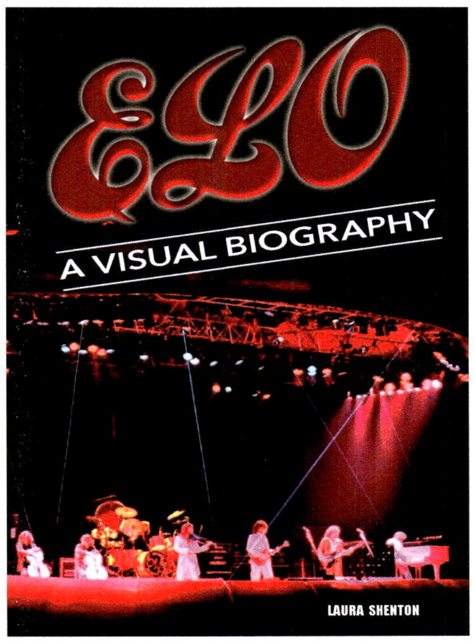
ELO
A VISUAL BIOGRAPHY
LAURA SHENTON

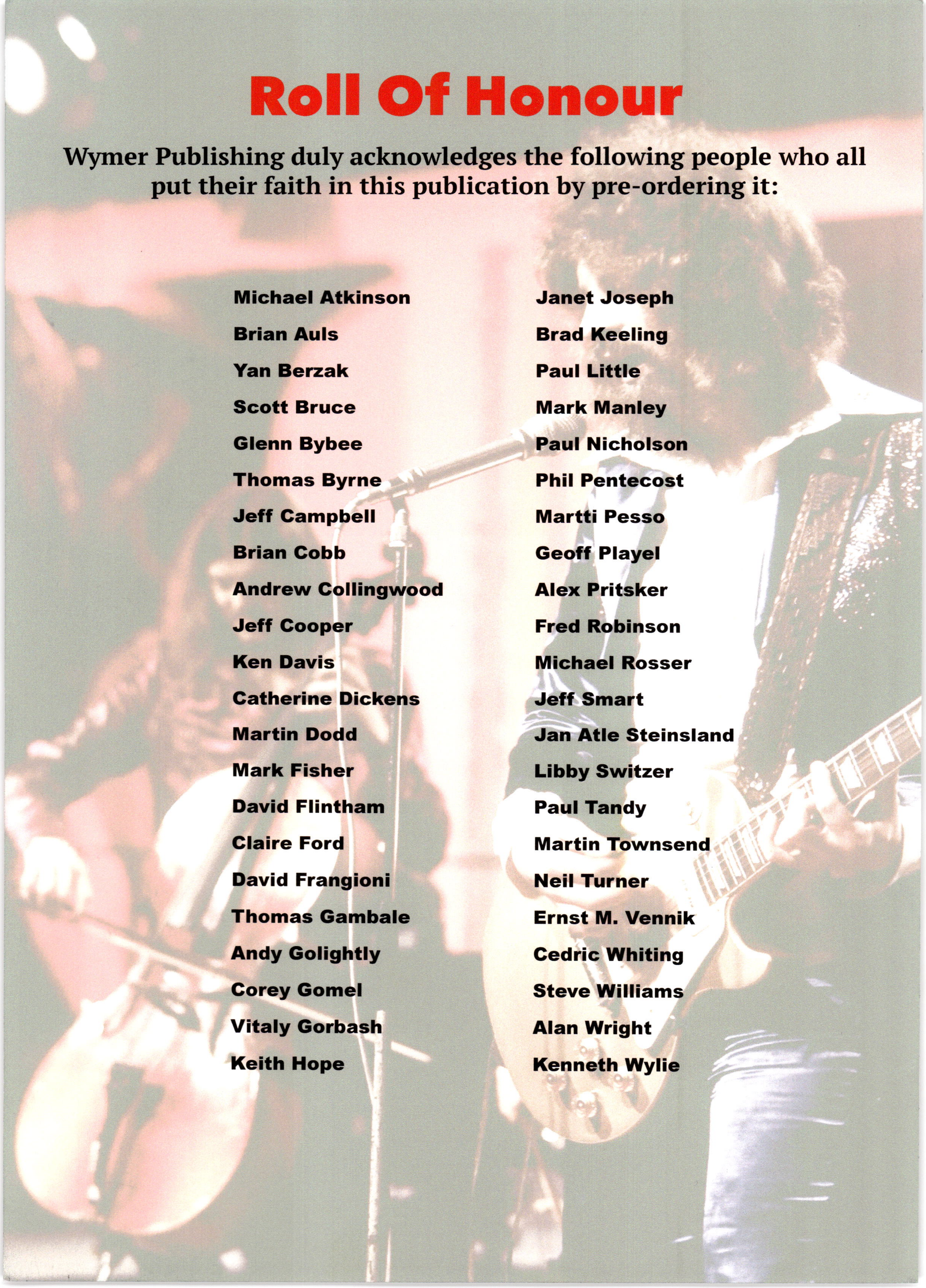

Roll Of Honour

Wymer Publishing duly acknowledges the following people who all put their faith in this publication by pre-ordering it:

Michael Atkinson
Brian Auls
Yan Berzak
Scott Bruce
Glenn Bybee
Thomas Byrne
Jeff Campbell
Brian Cobb
Andrew Collingwood
Jeff Cooper
Ken Davis
Catherine Dickens
Martin Dodd
Mark Fisher
David Flintham
Claire Ford
David Frangioni
Thomas Gambale
Andy Golightly
Corey Gomel
Vitaly Gorbash
Keith Hope
Janet Joseph
Brad Keeling
Paul Little
Mark Manley
Paul Nicholson
Phil Pentecost
Martti Pesso
Geoff Playel
Alex Pritsker
Fred Robinson
Michael Rosser
Jeff Smart
Jan Atle Steinsland
Libby Switzer
Paul Tandy
Martin Townsend
Neil Turner
Ernst M. Vennik
Cedric Whiting
Steve Williams
Alan Wright
Kenneth Wylie

In the annals of music history, there exists a band whose name alone conjures a symphonic kaleidoscope of sound and a visionary blend of rock and orchestration. Welcome to the enigmatic world of Electric Light Orchestra (ELO). With a career spanning decades and a sound that defies categorisation, ELO has carved its place in the pantheon of musical innovation. Like sonic alchemists, they transformed the familiar notes of rock into an electrifying fusion of classical grandeur and futuristic whimsy.
This book is a celebration of their unparalleled achievements, a voyage through their timeless melodies, and an exploration of the band that dared to harmonise the past, the present, and the infinite possibilities of the future.

During their original thirteen-year period of creating music and touring, ELO achieved remarkable success. They sold more than fifty-million records worldwide and were honoured with nineteen CRIA (Canadian Recording Industry Association) awards, twenty-one RIAA (Recording Industry Association of America) awards, and thirty-eight BPI (British Phonographic Industry) awards.

Between 1972 and 1986, the band managed to land an impressive twenty-seven songs in the top forty in the UK, and fifteen songs in the top twenty on the US Billboard Hot 100. Notably, ELO holds a unique record for having the most Billboard Hot 100 top forty hits without ever reaching the number one spot. In 2017, the band received the ultimate recognition of being inducted into the prestigious Rock and Roll Hall of Fame.

For the generation who grew up in post-war era Birmingham, UK, amidst the city's industrial landscape, many young men were united by a shared ambition: to be in a band and make music that would resonate with their peers. It was within this atmosphere of determination, hope and creativity that the story of ELO began.

The Idle Race circa 1967.
(Pictorial Press Ltd / Alamy Stock Photo)

The Move in 1969. Roy Wood and Bev Bevan with Carl Wayne and Rick Price. This four-man line-up was only together between July 1969 to February 1970. Carl Wayne then left to be replaced by Jeff Lynne.
(Pictorial Press Ltd / Alamy Stock Photo)

In 1968, Roy Wood — a multitalented musician serving as the guitarist, vocalist, and songwriter for the band The Move — came up with a particular idea. He envisioned the creation of a new musical ensemble that would break the mould by incorporating classical instruments such as violins, cellos, horns, and woodwind, infusing a touch of classical grandeur into rock music. The goal was to carry the torch of innovation, building upon the groundbreaking work of The Beatles in a fresh and exciting direction.

For many bands cutting their teeth in the late sixties and early seventies, the influence of The Beatles loomed large. With albums such as *Revolver* (1966) and *Sgt. Pepper's Lonely Hearts Club Band* (1967) to their credit, The Beatles' pioneering sonic experiments, unparalleled songwriting prowess, and remarkable commercial success had left an indelible mark on the music industry. It's no surprise that many emerging artists sought to follow in those footsteps, hoping to expand upon the fab four's command of sonic innovation and achieve similar levels of critical acclaim and commercial triumph.

The Beatles, often under the guidance of producer George Martin, had embraced the power of blending classical and rock elements, experimenting with orchestral instrumentation, and pushing the boundaries of traditional rock music. Whilst Wood and co.'s music would exude a distinct Beatlesque influence, particularly in its lush, multilayered arrangements and harmonious melodies, the dedication to crafting a unique sound and the fusion of rock and orchestration would prove fruitful in the emergence of a unique musical identity.

Intriguingly, Wood aimed to shift the spotlight away from traditional guitars, the desire being to make the orchestral instruments the centrepiece of the music. This revolutionary notion piqued the interest of Jeff Lynne, the charismatic frontman of Birmingham band, The Idle Race. Initially, when Trevor Burton (guitarist and founding member) left The Move in February 1969, Lynne declined Wood's invitation to join the project. He remained steadfast in his pursuit of success with his existing band.

Jeff Lynne, Bev Bevan and Roy Wood as The Move in 1971. Performing 'Tonight' on West German TV channel ZDF's music programme, *Disco*.
(Arthur Grimm / United Archives GmbH / Alamy Stock Photo)

However, fate had other plans. In January 1970, when lead singer Carl Wayne decided to part ways with The Move, Jeff Lynne seized the opportunity and accepted Wood's second invitation. There was just one condition: their collective energies would need to be wholeheartedly dedicated to this innovative and uncharted musical venture.

In July 1970, Roy Wood introduced a significant change to a song composed by Jeff Lynne, originally intended to serve as a B-side for The Move. This marked the moment when their innovative musical vision began to take shape, and '10538 Overture' was born as the very first ELO track. Initially, the plan had been to conclude their involvement with The Move after the release of the band's *Looking On* album by the end of 1970, transitioning entirely to their new musical endeavour in the upcoming year. However, to provide financial support for the budding band, they embarked on one final project with The Move, resulting in the album, *Message From The Country*. It was recorded alongside the extensive ELO sessions and was released in mid-1971.

New Musical Express reported in early October 1970; "Roy Wood's ambitious plan to augment The Move into a ten-piece ensemble named the Electric Light Orchestra has at last been realised. The project — first reported in the NME last year — finally reached fruition this week with the news that the enlarged outfit is currently rehearsing and routining. The line-up includes a string quartet, French horn and two miscellaneous instrumentalists — plus Jeff Lynne on piano and lead guitar; Roy Wood on bass, acoustic guitar and oboe; and Bev Bevan on drums. Main function of the new orchestra will be for concert appearances, and it is expected to undertake a series of dates in this country towards the end of the year, when it has a sufficiently large and well-rehearsed repertoire. The band will also record, and its first release is expected to be an album. It is, however, stressed that The Move will continue to operate as a small group. In fact, it has a new single scheduled for release by Regal Zonophone next Friday (9th) — the Roy Wood composition, 'When Alice Comes Back To The Farm'. A new Move album will follow in mid-November."

Electric Light Orch's debut will be in Feb.

THE long-awaited live debut of the Electric Light Orchestra has at last been scheduled! It was announced this week that Roy Wood's ambitious brain-child will make an extensive tour of Britain and Europe, starting in February and lasting a minimum of five weeks. Home dates in London and key provincial cities are at present being set.

A cellist has now been found to complete the personnel of the ELO, and full-scale rehearsals have begun this week. Founder members Roy Wood, Jeff Lynne and Bev Bevan have now completed all their live commitments as the Move, which will in future only be represented in record form.

A 35-minute colour film, tracing the transition from the Move to the Electric Light Orchestra, has now been completed and is at present being edited. It is to be generally released on the EMI circuit to coincide with the outfit's debut tour.

MOVE OVER FOR THE ELO

THE FIRST love in Roy Wood's life is obviously his new 10-piece mini-orchestra, the ELO, but meanwhile the Move are apparently still alive and very much kicking with their new single "California Man", which is another of his brilliant early rock distillations put through a space-age sound box.

WOOD: visual impact

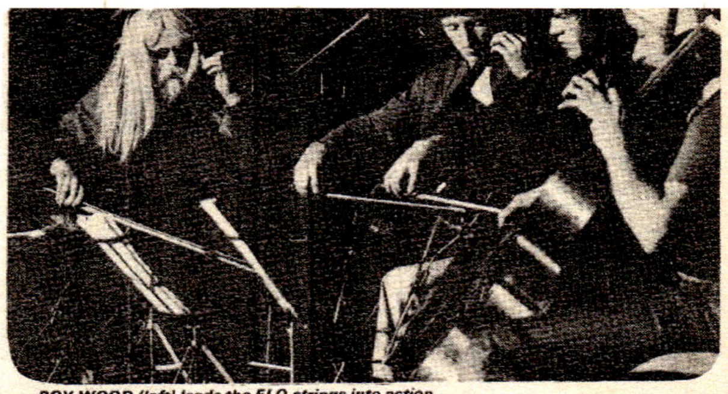

ROY WOOD (left) leads the ELO strings into action.

by KEITH ALTHAM

While one concept is a completely unique musical innovation, the other is just as obviously geared at making money from smart snappy singles.

There then arises the question as to whether anyone can expect to have the best of both worlds — original contemporary music and top pops?

At their manager Don Arden's London office recently we discussed the problems of the musically-split personality with the nucleus of Roy Wood, Jeff Lynne and Bev Bevan, who provide the motoring force for both bands.

"It's obviously going to be confusing to some people," said Wood, "but without the Move there would be no ELO. We could never have got a record company to back us on a project which was so unusual. There is no precedent for ELO because it is something completely new and without comparisons. People find it very difficult to assess us.

"With ELO we're really not trying to do anything that anyone has done before and we're breaking new barriers all the time. I think people really appreciate that fact, and they've been kind to us. ELO is the thing with which Jeff, Bev and myself are most deeply concerned, and that is the working band for which we want recognition. The Move hasn't really worked as a live band for 18 months and we have no plans for it to work again!

"I don't think anyone has operated on the kind of split level that we do at present, but we've proved that you can do it.

"Sure, we're confusing a few people who might think in terms of the Move, but we're also turning them on to our new work — we get a few shouts of 'Blackberry Way', but on the whole the audience know we are trying to do something different and are very appreciative.

"You have to remember that people were confused when they first heard the Beatles. When I first heard 'Love Me Do' I thought they must be trying the Four Preps or something. It was very weird. Pioneering is always a difficult trip."

Money

Bevan, who appears to be the group's financial head, emphasised that the band is really a labour of love, and that by virtue of their number and the heavy overheads they cannot expect to [illegible] a lot of money out of live [illegible]arances.

"It costs us approximately £200 in travelling expenses, roadies and wages before we even get on the stage," he said. "If we have to hire the hall, if we are promoting, you can almost treble that figure. But we're prepared to lose a little money in the experimental stages of the band.

"One problem is that people have a preconceived idea of what the Move are, and it prejudices opinion about ELO. We have to break down that pre-conception.

"But the ELO was primarily aimed at the American market, and that's where we hope to make our real break-through. In America they thought of the Move in a kind of 'underground' concept anyway, which takes us right away from those pop comparisons which people inevitably make in England."

Jeff Lynne enthused about the record company support for their forthcoming American trip. In the States they are marketing various ELO goodies, such as display boards which light up with bulbs and special giveaway ELO light bulbs.

"We're now awaiting a call from Osrams to do a commercial," Lynne smirked. "Can't wait for that — I've always used Osram," he boomed. "Used to eat them as a kid for breakfast. Once I got one I saved up for the set."

Having contributed that much to the interview he made his excuses: "Got to go now, I'm doing a session for Marc Bolan." He was a little put out when I didn't believe him at first. It appears he and Bolan are good friends.

I returned to talking about ELO's 10-man personnel, and how the members were chosen.

"It was really just a case of getting the best musicians available," said Wood. "Bill Hunt and Richard Tandy are Birmingham lads and the others are just the best Musician's Union guys we could find. The other guys are on wages because that's they way they wanted it, but we're beginning to settle down more as a band and get to know each other.

"America is likely to be the big test for us because living together on the road out there for six weeks really proves whether you're friends or not.

Theatrics

"We hate 'em all really," said Wood with a grin. "No don't put that down, they're still at the stage where they believe everything they read in the papers.

"Christ, he's put that down as well," said Bevan, observing my notes.

One thing that Wood has taken with him from his Move performances is the theatrics in terms of his somewhat bizarre costume — coming on stage as an old man in a long white wig with dark glasses is right in character for the man who likes to be out of character.

"It's kind of Marc Bolan in reverse," he explained with a smile. I just did it to be different.

"We obviously have to give people some sense of identification, and visual communication helps as much as anything. We also throw in a few rockers like 'Great Balls Of Fire' to get people going, and Jeff has written a few beaty things to give pace to the act.

"Perhaps people don't realise all the problems there are in amplifying all those string instruments we have — we're still sorting them out. It's one thing to dub them on the album and quite another sorting out the balance on stage.

"We're still improving and just about through the experimental stage, which is why I'm looking forward so much to doing the next album.

"The first album was a question of using any musicians available or doing it all ourselves, but this will be the band as it is on stage live — an entity.

"I had one plan to do a 'Lost Planet' story, but I'm shelving that for another album and we'll just concentrate on individual pieces."

Will the final acceptance of ELO mark the death of the Move altogether on record?

"Probably," said Wood, "but we'll cross that bridge when we come to it.

"I think it would be an enormous temptation to put out a Move single if we had material of that type about," added Bevan. "It's silly to just let it waste. I mean, we still get a lot of fun out of the Move."

One final thing to look out for from ELO is their own label, coming out in about two months time — for some strange reason they wanted to call it Auntie Sponnet or Uncle Turvis but the distribution company did not like the idea.

First artist on the label is Big Al from Birmingham with his Devil Canyon Rock and Roll band. Wood and his gang are currently mixing the album.

"He's an amazing talent," said Roy. "He's a huge rocker and he plays an old Fender Stratocaster which looks like a little spoon on his massive chest."

Look out — Big Al is coming.

MOVE TO STOP LIVE WORK; E.L.O. TO TOUR

THE Move will never again appear on stage in its own right, according to a spokesman for the group. But the Electric Light Orchestra, of which the Move is an integral part, is to begin a series of concert appearances at the end of September after months of preparation. The ELO's first album is now almost completed and will be released next month. Meanwhile, the search for a bass player for the outfit is expected to be resolved " within a few days."

Jeff Lynne told the NME this week that he could not foresee the possibility of the Move ever touring again in its present form. And this statement was confirmed by fellow group member Bev Bevan. (See also feature on page 4).

Electric Light Orchestra for live debut before year ends

THE MOVE plays its final date before concentrating solely on the Electric Light Orchestra at Yardley Swan on October 13, in aid of Birmingham City footballer Ray Martin's testimonial — also appearing are Raymond Froggatt and the Idle Race. The ELO debut album is now scheduled for release in November, but no live dates have yet been set for the outfit, although a spokesman told the NME that it hopes to appear " before the end of the year."

ELO START TOUR

ROY WOOD'S Electric Light Orchestra set out on their debut British tour next week, opening at Birmingham Kinetic Circus on Thursday, March 9. A total of some 30 dates is planned by Aquarius Management, spread over a three-month period and running through into June. Eleven venues have so far been confirmed, including an appearance at London Rainbow Theatre, and are listed below.

JOHN & TONY SMITH present

E L O

ELECTRIC LIGHT ORCHESTRA

IN CONCERT

plus special guest stars

COLIN BLUNSTONE and F.F.Z.

COLSTON HALL	BRISTOL	MAY	2nd
DOME	BRIGHTON	"	3rd
CIVIC HALL	GUILDFORD	"	7th
DE MONTFORT HALL	LEICESTER	"	8th
FREE TRADE HALL	MANCHESTER	"	9th
CITY HALL	SHEFFIELD	"	10th
GUILDHALL	PORTSMOUTH	"	11th
GUILDHALL	PLYMOUTH	"	12th
FAIRFIELD HALLS	CROYDON	MAY	14th
MUSIC HALL	ABERDEEN	"	17th
CITY HALL	NEWCASTLE	"	18th
GREENS PLAYHOUSE	GLASGOW	"	19th
EMPIRE	EDINBURGH	"	20th
CIVIC HALL	SOLIHULL	"	22nd
WINTER GARDENS	BOURNEMOUTH	"	23rd
PUBLIC HALL	PRESTON	"	26th

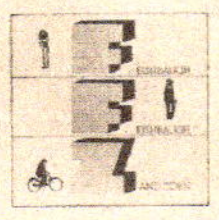

THE ELO (LEFT TO RIGHT) JEFF LYNNE, BEV BEVAN AND ROY WOOD

Roy Wood on the Move, ELO and Birmingham City's promotion chances

WITH almost schoolboyish enthusiasm Roy Wood squatted on the wooden steps leading up to the stage in the Royal Academy of Music and talked incessantly about the Electric Light Orchestra, his four-year-old brain child.

"It was about the time of 'Fire Brigade' that I first got the idea of the ELO and we've been getting it together for the past three years."

Roy was talking in a darkened corner of the room set aside for their London reception and debut last Tuesday. He had arrived almost two hours late, after missing his train from Birmingham, ready to explain why their London debut had to cancelled that same day. "Our mixer broke over the weekend and as it was custom-built to our own sound engineer's specifications we couldn't really borrow one. It's a real disappointment."

With a certain amount of reluctance I asked him about the Move, a name best whispered these days as the ELO pick up more and more publicity, good reviews and album sales. "They are what's keeping us going at the moment. Financially the Move singles are essential to the ELO. It costs a lot to run the orchestra, we have to pay our six classical members £15 per day just for rehearsals.

"We try and keep the two bands as far apart as possible. I write in two totally different ways for the Move and the ELO, always conscious of not putting strings on a Move record in case it comes out like the ELO, and keeping saxes out of the ELO."

For the three years they have been concentrating on the ELO, Move men Wood, Jeff Lynne and Bev Bevan have never really considered the possibility of killing off the hit-making Move band. "We are under contract for another three years with the Move so we can't really get rid of them. The only way it is possible is for the ELO to become so big that they outgrow and outsell the Move, so making them defunct," explains Wood.

Jeff Lynne, former Idle Race man, was, with Wood, the prime mover in the formation of the ELO. "At first," says Roy, "he didn't want to join the Move. They had a pop image and the Idle Race had an underground image which Jeff liked. It was only the plans we had for the ELO that swayed him.

"When I first got the idea I thought of arranging classical numbers as I wanted them but then I thought that I could write my own and Jeff came to mind. He lived nearby and I thought 'There's a great composer down the road'."

With as much tact as I could muster I asked Roy about the resemblance between his "1st Movement" track on the album and Mason Williams' "Classical Gas." "Yeah, it's a copy. I used to sit in the dressing room and play 'Classical Gas' and think it would be nice to write something like it, so I did. If you listen to it you'll notice that in fact they are two different tunes played in the same style."

Being back on stage with the ELO is almost like starting all over again for the band and fortunately they have been well received, even getting encores, on their first gigs.

"It's been a long time since we got encores on stage, even with the Move," says Roy. "Really the whole thing has given me a new lease of life. The Move would probably have just gone on making live appearances on the same old circuit for ever and ever, selling a few singles here and there and never any albums."

Forming the ELO has meant a lot of work for Roy, Jeff and Bev learning new instruments and new styles of playing. Roy has mastered the oboe, cello and almost the bassoon but not without problems. "It all takes a long time and you have to be good because the guys we are playing with know when you're crap."

Bev Bevan, drummer of long standing explains his problem. "It's a whole new concept for me and I'm enjoying it more than ever I did with the Move. These fellers are so good you can't afford to make mistakes."

Jeff Lynne, responsible for the majority of the tracks on the album and a principal conductor is more than pleased with the initial reaction to the orchestra. "It's lifting off nicely but it'll be about ten more gigs before we are really at our best. The American interest is good too and we are looking forward to going over later in the year."

'The whole thing has given me a new lease of life'

But before that trip there is another album lined up. "It's supposed to be ready in September," says Roy, "but it's going to be a bit of a rush. I've got an idea for it called "The Lost Planet" with the album based on one theme about this guy in years to come whose job each day is to go out and search for the lost planet and each track will represent what happens to him and what he sees and meets in his search."

Another project close to Roy's heart is his own solo album which he has completed. "I don't know when it's coming out, I've still got to do the cover design. It's made up of a few songs I had that didn't fit either the Move or the ELO and rather than leave them on the shelf, I thought I'd stick them out.

"It was done half for fun really but I think I'd like to do it again but I don't see myself going out on the road as a solo artist."

Plans for the ELO in the future include the addition of new members and Roy has a fancy for a brass section. "It's an obvious move really, I'd like to get a row of saxes going like the old Rock-n-Rollers but with the cellos in the background."

Spoken of as a genius now, Wood is out to perfect the fusion of pop and classical music. "There is a perfect fusion, we haven't done it yet and we may never do it but we'll keep trying at it. In the past the fusion has always consisted of an orchestra and a rock band joined but still independent of each other. We decided to get together and become much closer."

The nine-piece ELO, ten including sound man Trevor Smith, has got off to a good start but Roy sees the big test coming when they play Birmingham. "All our mates will be coming along and staring at us, waiting for us to make a mistake. It'll be terrible."

Apart from the disappointment of not playing in London, Roy's biggest upset last week was missing Birmingham City's final home match of the season. "I really hope they get promotion, they should do. Coming down on the train all the heads were hanging down because we had to miss the match—it was a real drag."

Still there's consolation for them if City go up and ELO take-off. That'd be better than the FA Cup and League double.

BRIAN SOUTHALL

However, in September 1971, *Record Mirror* would go on to report; "The Move, who abandoned live work over a year ago in order to develop the Electric Light Orchestra, are making a one-date only comeback in mid-October. They headline at The Swan, Yardley, Birmingham, on 13th October." As part of the same feature, a spokesman for the group keenly emphasised; "This is definitely not the start of a series of dates by The Move. The Electric Light Orchestra will be under way by the end of the year."

One musician who was briefly in the fledgling ELO was Glenn Hughes (bassist and vocalist for the Midlands band Trapeze, who more famously went on to join Deep Purple in 1973). Hughes has gone on record as saying that the notoriously demanding Don Arden had intimidated him into joining the early line-up of ELO, before any live shows. He was involved for about two weeks until Arden got a call from Hughes' mother, Sheila, who was adamant that her son could not be in the band.

In recent years, Hughes recalled; "Up pulls a Rolls Royce and it's Don Arden who comes to ask me if I'd like to join a new band called ELO, and I said to him [puts on a timid childlike voice], 'Okay, I'll join. Where do I sign?'. Of course, I was too frightened to say 'no.' About two weeks later, my mother called Don Arden and said 'Don, he's not ready!' — so I joined ELO for about two weeks."

The debut ELO album, *The Electric Light Orchestra*, was given a UK release on Harvest Records in December 1971. The label had been created by EMI in 1969, its purpose being to market progressive rock, and to compete with Philips' Vertigo label and Decca's Deram (as well as the independent label, Island). Throughout the 1970s, Harvest Records would primarily release progressive rock recordings by British acts — amongst them were Pink Floyd, Syd Barrett, Kevin Ayers, Barclay James Harvest, Be-Bop Deluxe and Deep Purple.

POPS

JAMES BELSEY

How the Move saw the light

NEXT week sees the return of the Move to the Colston Hall in their new guise of the Electric Light Orchestra.

Few seem to have realised it, but the Move — the Birmingham group who have somehow managed to combine hit records with an Underground image — haven't really existed for two years.

Their records have consistely appeared in the charts in the meantime, but the three members, Bev Bevan, Jeff Lynne and Roy Wood, have only worked as a recording group who make the odd radio and TV appearance to plug their latest product.

Bev Bevan, who's been with the group since they were formed six years ago, said: "This concert tour is the first we've done for at least two years.

Original

"We stopped playing because the old Move was getting too undemanding and we wanted something with a bit more scope."

So the three members began auditioning classical musicians in their search for something original, and some months ago they hired a pianist, french horn player, cellist and violinist.

"We wanted to explore music with a classical approach. But not just a series of "lifts" from classical music. It's been a long job," Bev said.

"To start with, balancing up their instruments was difficult. Try to get a violin to get the same volume as an electric guitar."

Then there was the problem of fitting in the classical approach to a rock sound, but the ELO has succeeded to everyone's satisfaction and a few days ago the concert tour began. It has been a great success so far.

Bev confessed: "It's worked very much better than we thought possible and some of the numbers are going down ridiculously well. On our first night we had three encores. so things are looking good."

The ELO unveil their classical rock to Bristol on Tuesday night.

Orchestra light on fans

Colston Hall, Bristol: Electric Light Orchestra.

One vital ingredient was missing at the Colston Hall last night — an audience big enough to set the place alight.

The Electric Light Orchestra, Colin Blunstone and FFZ played some of the most fascinating and original music staged in a Bristol rock show this year, but a mere 400 turned out to hear them.

It's not difficult to see why. The Move — now with six classical musicians under the ELO title — haven't played live for two years and so the word will have to get around about their stage performance. Once it does, the ELO must be one of this country's biggest attractions.

Because the sheer impact of their music from amplified cellos, violin and french horn behind a standard rock group line-up was electric, visually and musically.

Jeff Lynne and Roy Wood gave the pace with sharp, vivid vocals and the band's back-up was an explosive cloud of switching sound.

Colin Blunstone, the soft-voiced singer who made his name with the Zombies in the Beatles era, also used a classical string section, but without amplification.

He's still a very nervous solo singer, despite his recent success with "Say You Don't Mind," but his nerves didn't detract.

FFZ, an American band with a lithe, attractive and very effective girl singer, opened the show the way pop shows should be opened. Instead of giving a first act warm-up, they put across rich, original rock.

The ELO, Blunstone and FFZ all showed enormous promise — and the good grace to play with flair and enthusiasm to a quarter-full hall.

JAMES BELSEY

In the US, ELO's album was released in March 1972 — on the United Artists label, under the title of *No Answer.* The album's name was a quirky choice, inspired by an amusing incident when a record company secretary tried to contact the UK company for the album's name, but received no response. She left a note that read "No answer".

ELO's first album features the trio of Roy Wood, Jeff Lynne, and Bev Bevan as core members. Bill Hunt contributed the French horn parts, and Steve Woolam lent his talents on the violin. The album stands out for its distinctive sound when compared to the later, more polished ELO albums crafted under Lynne's direction. This particular recording embraces a unique sonic landscape, characterised by an abundance of wind instruments and a fascinating substitution of guitar parts with robust, almost sawing cello riffs. The resulting effect gives the album an experimental quality that could be described as a fusion: baroque-and-roll. Notably, 'The Battle Of Marston Moor' emerges as the track most deeply influenced by the baroque genre, with its ornate and intricate musical elements. For the recording of this number, Wood assumed a multitude of roles, playing nearly all the instruments himself, including percussion. This was necessary because Bev Bevan declined to participate on this particular track. His reluctance stemmed from his unfavourable opinion of it.

Released as a single in summer 1972 with 'First Movement (Jumping Biz)' on the B-side, '10538 Overture' achieved substantial success, reaching number nine in the UK. *Record World* keenly prophesised: "This superb and highly commercial British group will have an American hit sooner or later. This, the opening track from their new concept album, may be the one."

AQUARIUS presents at the
LIVERPOOL STADIUM
To-morrow (Sat.) 7.30 p.m.
ELO
(ROY WOOD, BEV BEVAN,
JEFF LYNNE, etc.)
Tickets 60p from Cosmopolitan

MANCHESTER EVENING NEWS, Friday, June 9, 1972

POP SCENE

Above: The English Light Orchestra—The Move, plus seven players from the LSO.

Moving on

A DOUBLE-BASS player with all the excitement and vitality of the Fifties' style of rock has caused a sensation with his cavortings on the Top of the Pops TV show.

Phil Copestake is the musician and his appearance with The Move as they perform their California Man hit, has fulfilled for him a life-long ambition. He always wanted to appear with the group on television, but he didn't get his chance until the California hit came along. For Phil is not a member of The Move — he is their road manager and he got the television spot because of his authentic-looking stage actions.

He plays the bass lying on his back, upside down, and in various other unorthodox poses as was the style in the heyday of Bill Haley's Comets, who were the stars of rock presentation.

"We made the disc as a tribute to rock," Move drummer Bev Bevan told me. "It was not done tongue in cheek. But we are amazed at the record's success — we didn't think it was all that catchy.

"Roy Wood wrote the number because we thought our music was getting too soft. We wanted to be lively."

The group — Bev, Roy on guitar, and Jeff Lynne on piano — have certainly achieved that with California Man. They appear in drainpipe trousers, bootlace ties, and all the Fifties' gear.

"But that is only for the television appearance," Bev assured me. "We don't dress like that off stage. I'm too young to remember Bill Haley and all the other originals, but I have seen film of them since."

Despite the success of the current single, The Move do not plan to appear live for concerts. "It's two years since The Move played a live gig," said Bev. "And we have no plans in that direction."

Instead the group are channelling all their output into the Electric Light Orchestra, a 10-man group they formed with the addition of seven London Symphony Orchestra musicians. The ELO is directed at integrating rock and symphonic music, and is this week on tour in Italy. In August they go to the United States, where their album, ELO, has just broken into the charts.

"I felt lost as the drummer in the ELO at first," confessed Bev. "I was not used to the orchestrations; it was more difficult."

But now he has mastered the technique and the group has gone from strength to strength. And, ironically, California Man will help their progress. Cash from the record will go towards financing the ELO project.

Will the three-man Move group ever appear live again? "Not if the Electric Light Orchestra becomes a big success," said Bev. "That is where our musical direction lies now, although The Move will still make records."

PICTURED FOR the first time: Roy Wood's Electric Light Orchestra, currently in the middle of its first concert tour. (L to r) Roy Wood (guitar and vocals), Wilf Gibson (violin), Richard Tandy (bass), Hugh McDowell (cello), Trevor Smith (sound), Jeff Lynne (piano nd vocals), Phil Copestake (tour manager), Bev Bevan (percussion), Andy Craig (cello), Richard Battle (roadie); Bill Hunt (French horn).

DE MONTFORT HALL LEICESTER
Manager: T. B. GODDARD, D.M.A.
MONDAY, 8th MAY at 7.30 p.m.

JOHN & TONY SMITH present

ELECTRIC LIGHT ORCHESTRA
IN CONCERT

PLUS SPECIAL GUEST STAR
COLIN BLUNSTONE
AND F.F.Z.

TICKETS: 75p 65p 50p 40p
Bookable in advance from MUNICIPAL OFFICE, Charles Street, Leicester. Tel.: 27632.
Open 9-30 a.m. to 5 p.m. (12 noon Saturdays).

Postal Booking Form — Electric Light Orchestra
To MUNICIPAL BOX OFFICE.
For the 7-30 p.m. perf. on Monday, 8th May.
Enclose stamped addressed envelope and P.O./Cheque value £ . p.
(Please delete words not applicable)

Date ....
Please forward .... tickets at ....
Name ....
Address ....

Printed by Electric (Modern) Printing Co. Ltd., Manchester

Both Roy Wood and Jeff Lynne lent their vocal talents to '10538 Overture'. The song's narrative revolves around an escaped prisoner. As part of this, Lynne had a distinctive idea: he wanted to assign a number — rather than a name — to the character in the song. During the process, while gazing at the mixing console, he stumbled upon the number "1053". To better suit the song's melody, Roy Wood proposed the addition of an "8".

"After recording the basic backing track, the other guys went home, leaving Jeff and myself to run riot with the overdubs," recalled Wood. "At the time, I was very keen on collecting instruments, and had just acquired a cheap Chinese cello. After we had finished overdubbing the guitars, I sat in the control room trying out this cello and sort of messing around with Jimi Hendrix-type riffs. Jeff said, 'That sounds great, why don't we throw it on the track.' I ended up recording around fifteen of these, and as the instrumentation built up, it was beginning to sound like some monster heavy metal orchestra. In fact, it sounded just bloody marvellous."

"I had this guitar track, like a real big riff on a guitar," said Lynne. "I laid it down in the studio and Roy Wood got his cello, his Chinese cello, and he overdubbed about fifteen cello riffs, just double-tracking all the time — and it sounded fantastic. We thought, it was like 'Wow!' and we just sat round playing it for days."

An instrumental composed by Wood, 'First Movement (Jumping Biz)', which also features on the debut album, showcases his talents on classical guitar, oboe, and cello. Interestingly, Wood has openly acknowledged that the track drew inspiration from Mason Williams' 1968 hit song 'Classical Gas'.

'Mr. Radio' had initially been planned as the second single to be released from *The Electric Light Orchestra*. However, this didn't transpire. It was on the 2005 compilation album, *Harvest Showdown*, that the edited single version of the song was finally released.

Live orchestral rock proves over-ambitious

ROY WOOD must be living a somewhat schizophrenic existence at the moment. You may have seen him and his band, the Move, cavorting and jiving to their new single, the rock and roll parody "Californian Man", on "Top of the Pops". But last night he appeared at Leicester's De Montfort Hall for a concert in a rather more serious vein with his Electric Light Orchestra.

Wood, one of the most creative minds in British pop, has attempted to intigrate amplified string instruments within a traditional rock group frame work. It is not a new concept of course — Denny Laine tried it with his ill-fated Electric String Band — but the Move man feels that his venture is taking the technique used by the Beatles on "I Am the Walrus" to its logical conclusion.

He has spent three long years finding the right musicians with classical training, perfecting the amplification and writing suitable material for the fusion.

Judging from last night's performance, I can see that Wood is aiming for that rolling orchestral rock featured on records like "Classical Gas" and "McArthur Park." But these were cut inside a studio, and I can't help feeling that he's being over-ambitious in trying to re-create this style on stage.

Weak material

There were times last night when the bizarre ensemble really clicked, with the bank of earphoned cellists producing a heavy, intense wave of sound punctuated by Jeff Lynne's stylish guitar and underlaid with Bev Bevan's driving percussion. When it worked the ELO was an uplifting experience, something quite unique in avant garde rock. But sadly such moments were few and far between.

For the most part it was a discordant cacophony with Wood striving to keep the two factions together and generally failing. If anything the material was rather weak and didn't really lend itself to the concept. Certainly the inclusion of Jerry Lee Lewis' "Great Balls of Fire" was a tragic mistake.

However, I'm not entirely pessimistic. Wood is an astute artist who will salvage something worthwhile from the venture. I just feel he's been a little premature.

Colin Blunstone, former lead vocalist of the Zombies who now fronts his own band, provided tasteful support with his programme of poignant, introspective songs sung in a husky, half-whispered style. He could well make it on his own. — **P.B.**

Move? E.L.O.? Wizard?

Once upon a time music used to be very easy. A record would be released by Freddy Shreddie and the Wheatyflakes and you would know that it was *the* Freddy Shreddie and no-one else was involved.

Therefore if you liked him you would buy his record and pay special attention to his next release. Nothing could be easier.

But to-day things are different, and an excellent example of how much different is the ever-continuing saga of the Move, or the Electric Light Orchestra, or Wizard.

But let's start from act one, scene one. In the beginning there was the Move, a band from Birmingham who made a great impression by their music and stage act which included the destruction of televisions, fridges and effigies of people.

The group was made up of Roy Wood, Bev Bevan, Jeff Lynne and Carl Wayne. Then, after Wayne's departure Roy Wood decided to set up a band called the Electric Light Orchestra which consisted of himself, Lynne, Bevan and a few other guys filling in on 'cello, bass and other kindred instruments.

While the E.L.O. was playing and recording the Move, in the persons of Wood, Bevan and Lynne, also continued to play and record.

Electric Light Orchestra — 10538 Overture/1st movement (Harvest)

Roy Wood, having taken Move up the charts, now turns his attention to Electric Light Orchestra, and this is the lead track from their first album.

The "A" side smacks of latter day Beatles and grows on you.

RECORD MIRROR, June 17, 1972

MOVE, ARGENT IN POP RIOTS

THE MOVE / Electric Light Orchestra manager, Don Arden, was arrested last Tuesday during the Electric Light Orchestra's concert at Padova.

"The trouble had started a day earlier, when wildly-excited crowds in Arezzo had created a near-riot.

"As a result of that," Don told RM, "the police in Padova were tipped off that they should expect trouble, and the concert hall was surrounded by police both inside and out a good three hours before the start of the show.

"In the middle of the fifth number, 'Great Balls Of Fire,' a man in shirt-sleeves asked me something in Italian. When I tried to explain that I was English and didn't understand, he became hysterical and grabbed my shirt, so I hit him. He turned out to be the chief of police, and he'd been trying to get me to call off the concert, thinking I was the manager of the concert hall.

"I don't think there was any justification for stopping the show – the kids were very excited but they weren't looking for trouble."

The concert was duly stopped. Amid riotous scenes, Don was arrested and detained for two hours questioning at the local police station. After his release, he took the 7.30 a.m. plane back to London, and stayed in Britain until Saturday night, when he flew back out to take charge of the E.L.O.'s last two concerts, at Viarregio on Saturday, and Milan on Monday.

Don Arden was not the only manager to hit out at the attitudes of the Italian police this week: Argent's Mel Collins condemned the use of tear gas by police at the Theatre Lyrico in Milan, after they had dispersed a 2,000 crowd following Argent's concert there.

Towards the end of the concert, which attracted a capacity audience, 50 riot police were called in in an attempt to calm down the wildly demonstrative fans. The group had played five encores, and the curtain had been brought down, but the audience still refused to go until the tear gas was used.

Said Collins, "There were absolutely no signs of impending violence. As far as I could see, it was a clear case of unwarranted police interference. The fans were noisy and enthusiastic, but using tear gas just wasn't on."

A riot was narrowly avoided at Dusseldorf, when Nazareth played there on Sunday night.

After the group had played a normal length set plus one encore, the promoter pulled out the plugs, enraging the audience of 10,000. After 10 minutes during which time the audience threatened to get out of hand, the promoter asked Nazareth to go back on, and they did a further 20 minutes. Peace was restored.

‘Queen Of The Hours’ holds the distinction of being the very first publicly released ELO track. Harvest Records unveiled it in November 1971 as part of a compilation, *The Harvest Bag*, which showcased several artists under the label.

The album artwork for *The Electric Light Orchestra* was crafted by the Hipgnosis design team of Storm Thorgerson and Aubrey Powell. The photos of the band adorning the back cover, where they are dressed in attire reminiscent of the seventeenth century, were taken at London’s Banqueting House. This creative choice not only contributes to the overall baroque aesthetic of the album but underscores the emphasis on the historical and cultural elements that permeate the record’s theme and overall identity. The Banqueting House, located on Whitehall in central London’s City of Westminster, stands as a remarkable and well-preserved example of the architectural style typical of banqueting houses, which were specifically designed for extravagant and lavish social gatherings. It holds the distinction of being the sole substantial remnant of the Palace of Whitehall, which was the primary residence of English monarchs from 1530 to 1698.

The Electric Light Orchestra got to number thirty-two in the UK. In the US, it only just scraped into the Billboard 200 chart at number one-hundred-and-ninety-six. It fared reasonably in Australia, where it got to number fifty-four.

One of ELO’s earliest performances took place on 16th April 1972, at the Greyhound Pub in Croydon, Surrey. Most ELO biographies state this as the debut gig, although it’s worth pointing out that a whole tour for April 1971 had been planned, but was cancelled. Likewise, the 1972 tour was supposed to start with a show at the Kinetic Circus in Birmingham on 9th March, but along with a handful of other dates in both England and Europe, they too were cancelled.

SUMMERTIME ROCK AT BRIDLINGTON SPA
Barry Nettleton presents for Circle
SATURDAY, SEPTEMBER 2nd
8 p.m.
ELECTRIC LIGHT ORCHESTRA
Only 60p.
SLADE—SATURDAY, AUGUST 26th.
BARS - FOOD - WHARFRAT MUSIC - LATE BUSES TO HULL
FREE CONCERT — EAST PARK, THIS SUNDAY, 1 p.m.
With STACKRIDGE, SNAKE EYE, SNIPS SHIVA, VENOM, etc.
SEE YA THERE.
WINTER GARDENS
WESTON-SUPER-MARE Tel. W-s-M 29512
Will patrons kindly note that although contracted to appear on
Saturday, September 9
SLADE
WILL NOT APPEAR
The Management have now contracted as replacement
THE ELECTRIC LIGHT ORCHESTRA
for this date.
Tickets : 70p in advance, 75p on the day
Refunds on tickets purchased for Slade will be made on production of the tickets not later than Friday, September 8. Personal callers at Box Office please.
Postal refunds on application to the General Manager, Catering and Entertainments Dept., Winter Gardens, Weston-super-Mare, together with tickets
NO REFUNDS CAN BE GIVEN ON THE DAY
Tickets purchased for Slade may be used for the Electric Light Orchestra
CIVIC HALL — GUILDFORD
SUNDAY, MAY 7th, at 7.30 p.m.
JOHN AND TONY SMITH present
ELECTRIC LIGHT ORCHESTRA
IN CONCERT
PLUS: Special Guest Star
Colin Blunstone and F.F.Z.
Tickets: 70p, 60p, 50p. Bookable in advance from: William Harvey Ltd., High Street, Guildford. Tel. 68171.

The line-up for the Croydon gig consisted of Roy Wood, Jeff Lynne, Bev Bevan, Bill Hunt (on keyboards and French horn), Andy Craig and Mike Edwards (both on cello), Wilfred Gibson (on violin), Hugh McDowell (also on cello), and Richard Tandy (on bass). It would prove to be a short-lived line-up. Tandy later went on to say that following the opening number of '10538 Overture', the songs the band played thereafter sounded hectic due to the confusion of changing between tunes. On the plus side, it made him consider that from there, the only way was going to be up.

That said, initial shows weren't always well received, or well-attended. For example, when James Belsey reviewed one of the earliest shows at Bristol's Colston Hall for the *Bristol Evening Post*, he was clearly enamoured with both ELO and the support acts Colin Blunstone and FFZ. He opined; "They played some of the most fascinating and original music staged in a Bristol rock show this year." But Belsey also reported that there were only four-hundred in the two-thousand capacity venue. Elsewhere, the *Leicester Mercury* took a less positive view of the music, citing it as over-ambitious.

Before the band really started to taste success, Andy Craig left, and shortly thereafter, during the recording sessions for ELO's second album, Roy Wood departed. He took Hunt and McDowell with him and went on to form his own group, Wizzard. Both Wood and McDowell cited issues with their manager, Don Arden, feeling that he had not fulfilled his role effectively (even though Wood retained Arden to manage Wizzard!). Additionally, they were dissatisfied with ELO's tour of Italy, where the cellos and violins struggled to be heard over the electric instruments.

WOOD QUITS ELO

Lynne taking over—official

ROY WOOD, who originated and founded the Electric Light Orchestra, is leaving the band and the leadership will be taken over by Jeff Lynne. The announcement was made by manager Don Arden last weekend, and confirms speculation reported in last week's NME. But Arden emphasised that the Move will continue to operate with Wood, Lynne and Bev Bevan as the nucleus of the group.

Said Arden: "Roy and Jeff are very talented composers and artists, but there comes a time when each deserves his rightful recognition. We all feel that, with Roy no longer in the ELO, Jeff will gain the recognition he deserves both as a composer and as leader of the group. Roy is going into something new and very exciting, which will be made known in the near future."

After the press conference, a slightly disappointed Wood said he had "no real choice" in leaving ELO — though he admitted it was his own decision to quit because Press publicity had been directed towards him, when Lynne should have received some of the credit. This, he said, could have caused bad feeling in the band.

Wood now has plans to take his newly-formed band Wizard on the road. It is a seven-piece outfit comprising two drummers, two cellists, bass and piano — plus Wood himself on guitar, cello and oboe.

The ELO, under Lynne's leadership, is now engaged in an extensive period of rehearsals — though no announcement has yet been made regarding Wood's replacement.

ELO: second U.S. tour

FOLLOWING the success of their debut tour, the Electric Light Orchestra have been signed for a second American concert tour, which starts in New York on October 14.

The itinerary, basically concerts with a few college gigs, will last three weeks.

ELO returned from their American trip on Monday and play four British gigs this month. They are City Hall, Truro (tonight, Thursday), Queen's Hall, Barnstaple (tomorrow, Friday), Guildhall, Plymouth (Saturday) and Town Hall, Torquay (22).

During the final week in July, the band will complete a new single for mid-August release.

Jeff Lynne diplomatically said; "We are not sure why he quit. It came as a surprise to us when Roy left." Bev Bevan was more forthright when speaking to the press about Wood's departure. As he saw it, Wood was "embarrassed" for getting too much of the credit: "Whenever ELO was mentioned in the press, Roy's name was always linked with it. But it was Jeff who was really doing the work with the band. He wrote '10538' and most of the material on ELO's album."

Despite predictions from the music press that ELO would probably disband without Wood, Jeff Lynne assumed leadership. Bevan, Edwards, Gibson, and Tandy remained in the line-up, with Tandy transitioning from bass to keyboards to fill in for Hunt. They were joined by new members Mike de Albuquerque and Colin Walker, who took over on bass and cello respectively. This revamped line-up marked the beginning of a new chapter in ELO's evolution. The newly-formed line-up made its debut performance at the 1972 Reading Festival on 12th August.

The same month, Bevan re-appraised the Wood-less band: "We thought it was too dirgy with the old line-up. It made us feel uncomfortable on the stage. There were too many gaps between numbers while we changed instruments. With the new band, it flows. Actually, it was a boost to us when Roy left because we were getting lethargic about things and the old band was too big and we lacked direction. Roy's got a strong personality visually, but not when it comes to running a group. Roy doesn't throw his weight about."

KINETIC CIRCUS
MAYFAIR, BULL RING
021-643 2137
MONDAY, 7th February, at 8 p.m.
MOUNTAIN
Plus
JIMMY McCULLOCH BAND.
Advance Tickets 70p from usual agencies.
All enquiries 021-772 4731.
Coming soon—
ELECTRIC LIGHT ORCHESTRA
SHA NA NA.
FRIDAY, MARCH 2 at 7.30
Mel Bush presents
ELECTRIC
LIGHT
ORCHESTRA
£1, 80p, 70p, 60p
BOOBS
TIFFANY'S
Blackboy Hill
WED.,
23 AUG.
8-12 midnight
The
Electric
Light
Orchestra
Adm. 75p
SOUNDS — LITES — BARS
THE HARDROCK
MANCHESTER
Thursday, September 28th
ELECTRIC LIGHT
ORCHESTRA
with
QUINTESSENCE
8 p.m.
Doors open 7.00 p.m.
Thursday, October 5th
CURVED AIR
8 p.m.
Doors open 7.00 p.m.
Tickets available from:
HARDROCK BOX OFFICE, ONE STOP RECORDS
PAPER CHASE, HIME & ADDISON
The Hardrock Concert Theatre, Greatstone Road
Stretford, Manchester. Tel.: 061 6023/4

In early 1973, the band released their second album, *ELO 2*. This period also saw ELO making an appearance on the influential television programme, *American Bandstand*. Prior to getting to work on the second album, Bev Bevan had told a journalist, "Much of ELO will depend on the balance — we'll be able to feature many soloists that didn't get a chance on the first LP. It's very intricate music, arranged and written out by Roy and Jeff. It's very strict and nothing like The Move."

Released as *Electric Light Orchestra II* in the US, the band's second album was the last to be released on the Harvest label in the UK. Originally, the album was intended to bear the title The Lost Planet, but this concept was soon abandoned.

Although Wood had decided to part ways with the band during the creation of the album, he played cello and bass on two tracks: 'In Old England Town' and 'From The Sun To The World'. Notably, he wasn't credited for this upon the album's initial release.

Each of the album's five pieces exceed the standard rock song length and feature a rich, multi-layered orchestral instrumentation that contributes to a dense and intricate sonic experience (it features the band's lengthiest track, an anti-war song titled 'Kuiama'). Similar to its predecessor, *ELO 2* stands out as one of the band's less commercially orientated albums, although it did manage to get to number thirty-five in the UK, to number sixty-two in the US, and to number seventeen in Canada.

acoustic

Jeff Lynne and Mike de Albuquerque during the 1973 tour.
(Pictorial Press Ltd / Alamy Stock Photo)

San Diego appearance Nov. 21

Electric Light Orchestra: former comes on strong

ELECTRIC LIGHT ORCHESTRA
Biography

Crashing like a torpedo into the early days of 1973, a record called "Roll Over Beethoven" burst onto record charts. The song brought in a new twist in musical style with each succeeding verse. The Electric Light Orchestra had arrived in America. It will be in San Diego Nov. 21 at J.J.'s on Pacific Highway, San Diego.

Where they came from is a story requiring a little background. In 1965 there were many rock bands in the city of Birmingham, England. There were the Moody Blues, the Cheetahs, the Redcaps, Denny Laine & the Diplomats, Mike Sheridan & the Nightriders, Carl Wayne & the Vikings, and more.

In 1966 a new group was formed by members of some of these leading groups: The Move. The move was led by Carl Wayne and Roy Wood, and over the next few years they enjoyed a vast number of chart-topping English smash records. They were respected as much for their understanding of classic pop music structure as for their experiments in "underground" rock, and by 1972 were described as one of the world's best and most imaginative groups. Stereo Review picked them as the logical successor to the Beatles.

In 1970, amid changes in personnel, the Move was joined by Jeff Lynne, who years before had been a fellow member of Mike Sheridan's Nightriders with Roy Wood. His concepts of music were very similar to Wood's and together they conceived the idea for a group that would make not only the Move but everything else in rock obsolete: The Electric Light Orchestra.

"What I'd like to see happen," said then-member Carl Wayne, "is a complete pop orchestra. I'd like to get about five groups together, all good musicians, and take over the Royal Albert Hall for a concert. It'd start off with the whole ochestrra sitting down to play, and just the soloists standing to do their thing. But the whole concert would end with a complete maze of sound, with everyone blowing together. There would be a certain pattern to play to, but apart from that it would be free-form.... almost the ultimate in pop music."

Wayne subsequently left the group, and these theories were bent by Lynne and Wood, along with drummer Bev Bevan, to fit their conception of how pop music and classical themes could be joined. The first ELO album, No Answer, was released in mid-1972, and it worked up a momentum in its first year. Although the Move wasn't officially disbanded yet its personnel was the same as ELO with the addition of several guest soloists from the London Symphony Orchestra.

Following an initial tour of England, Roy Wood left the group to return to a more basic rock & roll sound, leaving ELO in the able hands of Jeff Lynne. Lynne made further changes, bringing in his friends from the Symphony on a permanent basis. The final lineup now reads: Jeff Lynne, guitar, vocals and Moog; Bev Bevan, drums; Wilf Gibson, violin; Mike Edwards, cello; Colin Walker, cello; Mike DeAlbuquerque, bass; and Richard Tandy, Moog, piano and guitar.

Although the Move had never been as successful in America as they were in England, they had built up a large and loyal following over the years — especially among rock writers and Anglophiles, who almost universally considered them their personal favorite pop underdogs. The debut of ELO was greeted with the same enthusiasm, their first album selling remarkably well for a first effort by an unknown group.

ELECTRIC LIGHT ORCHESTRA: SEATED, L. TO R., COLING WALKER, MIKE EDWARDS.
Standing, l. to r., Richard Tandy, Bev Bevan, Jeff Lynne, Mike DeAlbuquerque, Wilfred Gibson.

DISCORNER

WHETHER or not lovers of classical music would be too impressed by the fusion of rock and orchestration which many groups are employing these days, is debatable.

But unquestionably bands such as the Moody Blues and Deep Purple, who have both appeared with the London Philharmonic Orchestra in concert, have proved that the blend is very workable.

The Electric Light Orchestra surprised everyone with their unusual version of Chuck Berry's Roll Over Beethoven — and will no doubt do so again with their new album.

Simply entitled, The Electric Light Orchestra, the album includes five long tracks, three on the first side, and two on the second — a well balanced variety of straight rock and cello and violin work.

In Old England Town is one of the rockers with Jeff Lynne's guitar controlling the song completely.

There is a slight change with Momma, a gentler country number with more emphasis on harmony, and then follows a mammoth version of Roll Over Beethoven.

The band show their talents at orchestration on the reverse side and some whispering piano from Richard Tandy introduces From the Sun to the World (Boogie No 1).

Cynical

This track, and Kuiama, are almost entirely dependent on Mike Edwards and Colin Walker's cello work, Wilf Gibson's violin and Tandy's moog, piano and harmonium.

There is little guitar to break the mood, and although Lynne's lyrics are at times biting and cynical, it does not mar the intricate arrangement.

If any doubt, after hearing Roll Over Beethoven, the band's ability to play good music, they should listen to this album. (Harvest).

TUESDAY SCENE
by DEBORAH THOMAS

THE LIGHTER SIDE OF THE ELECTRIC

LIGHT RELIEF: from left, Colin Walker, Wilf Gibson, Mike Edwards.

ROLL over, Beethoven. The Electric Light Orchestra have put you on the pop scene again.

The weird and wonderful half-classical-half-pop group have turned Chuck Berry's song into a top ten smash hit in Britain.

"Roll Over Beethoven" originally sold a million for the big daddy of rock seventeen years ago.

Then the Beatles recorded it on their hit album "With The Beatles" in 1963.

Heavy

Now Beethoven has rolled up again.

The boys—whose stuff is mostly heavy—played "Roll Over Beethoven" as a bit of light relief on their recent tour of colleges and halls and found it "got 'em all at it," as founder member Jeff Lynne puts it. So they decided to release the number as a pop single.

But the hit makers would like us to take them seriously.

You won't catch these boys twanging a guitar in greasy denims and sweaty T-shirts. Cellos dominate their pop concerts and evening dress is a must on stage.

Guitarist Jeff Lynne, who's also a member of the successful The Move pop group, explains how such a bizarre band as the Electric Light Orchestra was formed.

"We got to hate bashing away at the same old thing night after night. We wanted to use nice instruments like cellos and violins."

So he and three pop friends joined three classical musicians to form the Electric Light Orchestra — ELO for short — in their spare time.

The two cellists, Colin Walker and Mike Edwards, and the violinist, Wilf Gibson, know all about Beethoven. They have performed with the London Symphony Orchestra and other top classical outfits.

Wilf has played under Andre Previn and Leonard Bernstein but, like the cellists, he became bored with the rigidity of the classical world and quit.

The LSO's loss was the ELO's gain.

Says Jeff: "They didn't need any persuasion to join us. They were right chuffed.

"They were dead straight at first. They read the dots on the score and didn't swear. Now they've changed completely. They play by ear and improvise as they go along."

The group's second album, called ELO 2, is out this week. It includes their latest hit but is basically a collection of serious works.

As for their next singles chart contender, Jeff Lynne promises a mini symphony.

Seriously, though.

Electric Light Orchestra Refreshing

By BRUCE MEYER
By United Press International

If anything ever kills off rock 'n' roll, it will be pretentiousness—the stuffed shirt attitude that puts phony artiness ahead of making people feel good. Rock music is meant to be enjoyed, not endured—but it's incredible how many bands don't know it.

There are exceptions, of course. The Moody Blues have managed to turn pretentiousness into an asset, while John McLaughlin's Mahavishnu Orchestra simply transcends all the labels that hold back ordinary mortals.

But the great mass of groups that have left the rock 'n' roll fold to play what has been laughably mislabled "progressive rock" end up meandering mechanically about in a foggy never-never land of tedious melodies and meaningless mystical lyrics.

A Refreshing Group

All of which makes it refreshing to come upon a group that can stretch the boundaries of rock—without departing them completely. Such a band is the Electric Light Orchestra.

A bit of history: The ELO is one of the offspring of The Move, a British band that was very successful in England, but just never made it on this side of the Atlantic, despite a couple of good albums.

The first ELO album, "No Answer" (United Artists S-5573) was a product of prime mover Roy Wood, and little more than a ponderous exercise in how not to combine classical music with rock—an example of the worst of "progressive rock."

Wood, apparently realizing he was in over his head, departed the ELO to start another band, Wizzard, and leadership of the ELO fell happily on guitarist Jeff Lynne.

No New Ideas

The new ELO album, "Electric Light Orchestra II" (UA-LA040-F), does not contain a single completely new idea. Lynne draws freely on all types of music, and has come up with a new way of putting them together.

There are only five tracks on "Electric Light Orchestra II," and four of them are excellent. The exception is the first cut, "In Old England Town," which sounds like a lead-winker reject from Sgt. Pepper-era Beatles album. It's almost as if Lynne felt he had to purge his soul of those dreary chords before moving on to happier things.

Besides the Beatles, there are three clear influences on the ELO: Classical, mellow country-rock (a la Doug Sham or The Band) and pure '50s rock 'n' roll. Lynne has a regrettable tendency to make his openings sound like movie themes, and he uses his moog synthesizer like an electronic tuba. But his dexterity as a musical juggler more than makes up for such weaknesses.

The High Point

There is absolutely no doubt about the high point of the album. It is the third track on side one, an eight-minute cut that opens with the ominous strains of Beethoven's Fifth Symphony—and slides gracefully into the raunchy riffs of Chuck Berry's "Roll Over Beethoven."

Now if someone had said a band was planning to make a big production out of that tune, with strings and all the trappings, I would have predicted disaster. But it was the only thing on the album, I'd still recommend it—it's got to become a rock classic.

If anything ever kills off rock 'n' roll, it won't be the Electric Light Orchestra.

ELO

THE Rainbow was far from full when ELO appeared, but the people who had turned up to see the Orchestra's concert seemed well pleased with what they offered.

Their sound was good and the individual musicians are all colourful and interesting, but it wasn't the best performance yet to come from Jeff Lynne's group. The 10538 Overture proved to be one of the best numbers, and they also featured I Might Be Dreaming and Paganini Blues, along with two up tempo jig compositions.

But really it was Thin Lizzy who shone the brightest. Each time they appear they seem to improve, and though the hall was something like only 25 per cent full when they played their set, they proved themselves to be a highly competent band. Look What The Wind Blew In opened the set, and the group built the atmosphere up to reach their Whisky In The Jar hit, and Down At The Farm. – A. G.

With their second album, ELO showcased their musical prowess with a grand eight-minute reimagining of Chuck Berry's 'Roll Over Beethoven'. Their remarkable rendition kicks off with a musical homage to Beethoven's Fifth Symphony, seamlessly integrating elements from the symphony's first movement into Berry's classic. It also references the *Peter Gunn* theme, which adds to a captivating tapestry of ideas. This iconic interpretation swiftly became one of ELO's signature songs, consistently serving as the closing piece for the majority of their live performances. With 'Queen Of The Hours' on the B-side, 'Roll Over Beethoven' got to number six in the UK, securing the band's second top ten hit. In the US, it got to number forty-two. The song's enduring appeal and innovative composition have left an indelible mark on ELO's legacy.

"There's a story about Beatles producer George Martin popping in to listen to ELO recording 'Roll Over Beethoven' at AIR Studios in 1972," Lynne recalled. "He was doing Paul's *Live And Let Die* in the studio next door, so he came in and gave 'Roll Over Beethoven' a thumbs-up. He actually sat and listened intently to it all the way through, because it was a bit of a strange arrangement with all those classical things in there. It was a great experience, and I got to know him a little bit then."

The UK and US versions of ELO's second album had notable distinctions. The UK album's cover, by Hipgnosis, features a painting of a light bulb voyaging through space, with the label 'ELO2' situated at the base of the bulb. In contrast, the US release had a different cover design, showcasing a more elaborate light bulb set against a nighttime backdrop.

Tops In Pops

Wizzard and Electric Light Orchestra are fraternal twins, difficult to tell apart though not quite identical. They are descendants of the Move, but they refuse to be as simple and direct as their respected ancestor, so they strike us as a bit unfamiliar and self-willed. But, though they don't sing about "cherry blossom clinics," they carry on a proud tradition of inspired madness, so we should watch closely their initial efforts.

"WIZZARD'S BREW"
By Wizzard
"ELECTRIC LIGHT ORCHESTRA II"
By the Electric Light Orchestra

Both groups are currently offering us albums which extend, exaggerate and often reduce to absurdity the kind of pounding, repetitive song that the Move put together expertly in its day. Both albums contain five long songs of seven to 14 minutes in length which are so similar in intent and structure that it is possible to see the two records as one double album with prime Mover Roy Wood in charge of one half and Jeff Lynne, the other creative force behind the Move, in charge of the other.

•

The distinctive feature of "Wizzard's Brew" is its raucousness. By contrast, "Electric Light Orchestra II" offers songs with an overall smoother sound. If you get the impression that the band is playing in a basement, that the musicians are crashing and clanging their way through each number, you know you're listening to Wizzard; if you hear a sweet-sounding violin or cello passage, it's the Electric Light Orchestra.

Now that we know which is which, how do we rate them? Unfortunately, a lot of the material on both albums is more exciting to think about than to listen to. The Electric Light Orchestra's "Roll Over Beethoven," a number which in many ways epitomizes the thrust of both records, is quite satisfying in concept. Here the group points out the essential idiocy of the original Chuck Berry song by recording it over a symphonic version of Beethoven's Fifth. But to carry on with the song for eight minutes after making the point in three is to strain the listener beyond the pleasure point.

Similarly the slightly off-key saxophone on Wizzard's "Buffalo Station" says a lot about all the "good old rock 'n' roll" bands, but the statement can't sustain our interest for a seven-minute exploration of one or two chords.

•

But there is more here than statement and the really fascinating tracks offer much to make the albums worthwhile. The archetypal great song in rock and roll is the slow-tempo love song which gives the singer the chance to move an emotional plea at his melodramatic best. Here Wizzard gives us "Wear a Fast Gun" which carries this sort of thing one step further. The lyrics, "Wear a fast gun and you'll be alright," are close to meaningless, but Roy Wood sings them with an intense mock sincerity which makes us imagine we are hearing the ultimate in ballads.

The tubas and strings carry us along in stately fashion to the emotional choral-singing climax at the end, and we laugh at the same time we marvel at Wizzard's expertise in putting the song together. On "Meet Me at the Jailhouse" Wood plays the most explosive riff imaginable on the bass strings of his guitar to introduce the song, and then proceeds to shout out the lyrics in the most absurd throat-wrecking manner. Again, we laugh at it and like it at the same time.

•

The Electric Light Orchestra offers us "Boogie No. 1" and "Boogie No. 2" (the full titles are too much). Both songs combine the power of electric guitars with that of cellos, violin sections and "classical" piano playing, and the group achieves a uniquely rich sound. Lynne's singing on "Mama" gives the song a color similar to "Wear a Fast Gun;" the lyrics do have their meaningful passages, though, and the total effect is less comic though equally pleasurable.

If "Wizzard's Brew" and "Electric Light Orchestra II" are somewhat less than perfect, they are nevertheless far above average. Furthermore, the fact that much of the music has an intellectual rather than an emotional appeal should not bother us. All music today is experimental, whether it is jazz, rock or avant-garde, and who's to say that it isn't the proper business of a rock band to musically comment on past styles and fads. All we can really say is that an artist must never bore his audience, and for the most part these artists don't bore us here.

TIM McKENNA

Starlight Room
GLIDERDROME
BOSTON

SATURDAY, 31 MARCH 1973

ELECTRIC LIGHT ORCHESTRA

DANCING 7 - 12 SUPPORTING BANDS BAR & REFRESHMENTS ADMISSION 60p

TOMBOLA Club Sessions : Tuesday & Friday commence 7.30, Sunday 7.

ELO — tour and single

THE ELECTRIC LIGHT ORCHESTRA – currently halfway through their second American concert tour – are to release a new single early next year to tie in with an extensive British and European itinerary.

The new single (a follow-up to the band's present chart success "Showdown") is almost certain to be "Ma Ma Ma Belle", written and produced by Jeff Lynne; scheduled release date is January 11.

The European itinerary is planned to begin in early February, and following two weeks of concerts in Holland, Belgium, Italy, Germany, France and the Scandinavian countries, the band will play a three-week British College and concert series taking them through to early March.

ELO will return to the US in the spring. The band return to Britain on December 20 — a week after the release here of their third album "And On The Third Day", scheduled for December 14 issue.

GRITTY FOOTNOTE: ELO played to over 22,000 people at an open air festival in Phoenix, Arizona, last weekend on a bill also featuring War and Three Dog Night. As the band completed their set, the arena was engulfed in a massive sandstorm, and the show was cancelled without the other bands playing a note!

formance at Brixton Prison's Annual Xmas Party on December 23.

The band are currently on a tour of the West Country. Dates as follows: Exeter, St. Luke's College (Dec. 7), Devizes Town Hall (Dec. 8), Swansea Patti Pavilion (Dec. 14), Burton On Trent 76 Club (Dec. 28).

Interestingly, for reasons that remain unclear, on the UK version of the album, 'Roll Over Beethoven' was slightly edited in length compared to how it appears on the US release. Additionally, the title of the second track, 'Momma', was adjusted to 'Mama' for the US — a worthwhile investment considering that audiences in the US were particularly welcoming towards ELO during this period. "I was really amazed by just how much American audiences knew about us before we went over for the first tour," said Lynne. "I mean, they were actually shouting out for numbers off the earlier albums along with things I'd done years ago with The Idle Race and The Move."

An instrumental rendition of the album's opening track, 'In Old England Town', was used as the B-side for the single, 'Showdown' (the band's last contemporary recording to be released on the Harvest label, it got to number twelve in the UK).

Whilst working on their third album, *On The Third Day*, ELO went through several line-up changes. Wilfred Gibson was dismissed, Mik Kaminski came on board as the new violinist, and Colin Walker left. Mike Edwards, the remaining cellist, took responsibility for completing the cello sections on the album.

On The Third Day was released in late 1973. It didn't chart in the UK, but it did reach number fifty-two in the US. Only the US version of the album features 'Showdown'. Also in late 1973, following his departure from Wizzard, Hugh McDowell returned to ELO as the second cellist. In certain regions, this return coincided with his appearance being used on the cover of *On The Third Day*, despite him not having contributed to the album's recordings. In particular, he is on the front cover of the US album — the unusual photograph of the band, displaying their navels, was taken by photographer Richard Avedon.

Electric Light scores

By JEANI READ

When you go around announcing that the music your band plays is going to make all other rock music obsolete, you'd better have something pretty incredible happening, or you're riding for one hell of a fall. But that's what the Electric Light Orchestra is doing, and after their concert at the Gardens Friday night it's easy to see why they're getting away with it.

They are bizarre in a beautifully original way, in a time when the bizarre itself is starting to suffer from overkill, bizarre in a kind of brilliantly controlled mania.

They know perfectly well that they'll never revolutionize anything, because probably only the Electric Light Orchestra can do what they are doing — imitations just won't make it. But the kind of music they do offer, when taken seriously, does provide a very viable alternative.

The whole beauty of the Electric Light Orchestra however is that they don't take it seriously — or maybe they do, who knows?

The Electric Light Orchestra is an outgrowth of a British band called The Move, and what they are doing now is taking a relatively conventional rock rhythm section — guitar, bass, drums, keyboards and synthesizer — and augmenting it with two cellos and violin, the latter abducted from the London Philharmonic. Classical and rock make an extremely unlikely combination but the Orchestra put them together with a confidence and ability that is really quite outstanding.

The old rocker Roll Over Beethoven is their current hit, but it sits comfortably in the set alongside the likes of Grieg, and it isn't just the superb musicianship and the ingenious handling of classical themes and rock rhythms or rock themes and symphonic embellishment that makes the Orchestra so impressive. It is their manner of presentation — they start deadpan and straight, simultaneously compelling and annoying, threatening to become outrageously pretentious. And then they subtly, imperceptibly, get to a point where cellos are played with oranges and violins seem in imminent danger of being sawed apart, and everything poises precariously, and hilariously, on the line between genius and insanity.

Electric light up the scene

THE ELECTRIC Light Orchestra's Bristol concert last night proved without doubt that this group are one of the brightest and most creative in Britain.

By today's standards, they are a curious combination for a pop group.

They have the usual four piece line-up of two guitars, drums and keyboards, with additional violin and two cellos.

But this odd mixture certainly pays dividends. This seven piece band are never out of the singles' and album charts.

Last night, they treated their Colston Hall audience to a strange mixture of classical rock, using a formula of past hits, classical pieces and tracks like the marathon On The Third Day, the title song from their latest album. T.D.

Exclusive contract

THE ELECTRIC LIGHT ORCHESTRA, Roy Wood's Wizzard and the Move recently signed an exclusive contract with Warner Brothers, and the first product, a new Light Orchestra album "On the Third Day" is to be released this month.

Wizzard are working on their debut Warner LP, while the Move are scheduled to complete at least one album a year.

The Electric Light Orchestra now consists of two Move veterans — the man who thought up the idea, Jeff Lynne and drummer Bev Bevan; Richard Tandy, Michael De Albuquerque on bass, and the string section, Mik Kaminski, Ted Blight and Mike Edwards.

On The Third Day contains shorter tracks than its predecessor, but the four songs on side one of the album were linked into a continuous suite. Mik Kaminski made his ELO debut on side one, but Wilfred Gibson features on side two. When Colin Walker left the line-up around the same time, it left Mike Edwards as the band's lone cellist.

'Ma-Ma-Ma Belle' was released as a single. In the UK, where it reached number twenty-two, the B-side was 'Oh No Not Susan'. The US version had 'Daybreaker'. *Cash Box* compared 'Ma-Ma-Ma Belle' to the style of rock and roll played by The Move: "Just take their [The Move's] brand of rock 'n roll, add an extra dash of heavy and there you have it — this new ELO disc." *Record World* called the single a "French-fried rocker" in which "crispy rock and roll should crunch onward as a bright biggie."

Bev Bevan said of the BBC's embracement of 'Oh No Not Susan'; "Jeff sings: 'Oh, no not me, that's all she says... her money and her place they just don't mean a fucking thing...' The BBC played it many times, despite their policy towards such lyrics. It just goes to show that if you keep quiet about it and don't make maximum fuss to get publicity, there isn't anyone listening closely to words on the radio."

POPCHAT

Album choice

ELECTRIC LIGHT ORCHESTRA'S Warner album "On the Third Day" is undoubtedly their best work to date. The sound effects and the string section are particularly effective, while the lyrics and vocals are handled in a very subtle way.

★ ★ ★

Performing on *Top Of The Pops* in 1974.
(Trinity Mirror / Mirrorpix / Alamy Stock Photo)

Jeff Lynne, vocalist, with the Electric Light Orchestra at the Colston Hall last night.

Only a glimmer of the real ELO

Colston Hall, Bristol: Electric Light Orchestra.

ELO, who've given two outstanding concerts at the Colston Hall in the last two years, barely scraped through this one.

The sound system was rotten, all muzzy edges and lost instruments, and the band weren't really playing to their usual form.

They salvaged their reputation with a last-minute burst of rock and roll, cellos pumping and guitars roaring and enough acrobatics around the stage to please the most jaded audience.

TALENTS

It may have been enough to please the customers, but it wasn't really enough to add anything to their reputation, as an original, creative unit who should be going places on the international scene.

The seven piece group specialise in a truly genuine mix of classical instruments and rock hardware. It's a fascinating idea and it usually works.

Last night Jeff Lynne put over some solid vocals and hard-driving guitar work with firm backings from his cellists and pianist Richard Tandy, but somewhere along the line the sound balance went astray and ELO's new violinist, Mik Kaminski, was often lost at key moments.

The lengthy "Queen of the Night" which should have been the show-stopper, seemed jerky and unrehearsed. The straightforward "Roll Over Beethoven" came over well, but it was a bit too easy for comfort, when you consider the group's many talents.

Raymond Froggatt, who opened the show, was stunning. He sounds like a toughened-up version of Joe Cocker and Leon Russell rolled into one, writes some superb music, and why he isn't a star I just don't understand.

JAMES BELSEY

LIVE

Electric Light Orchestra

SINCE THEIR formation a couple of years back the Electric Light Orchestra have had a series of problems prevalent from personal to musical confrontation.

Jeff Lynn's ambition to build a constructive unit capable of a wide melodious range has finally been realised to some degree as shown by ELO's performance at London's Theatre Royal, Drury Lane concert on Saturday.

It's obvious that three albums, a couple of American tours and hard rehearsing have given this seven-man outfit the confidence and ability to function well.

One tremendous asset has been the introduction of young violinist Mik Kaminski to the line-up whose visual and musical appeal surpass the talents of many in the group.

Jeff's still up front though but his "thank you very much" line after each number tended to be rather conservative on reaction after the sometimes hilarious stage capers of the string section.

The set comprised of old and new from hits such as Showdown and Roll Over Beethoven to material from ELO's new album, On The Third Day-one particularly nice piece as an interlude was the orchestra's version of Day Tripper with Richard Tandy doing a delightful piano melody.

I was a bit disappointed that the group didn't quite cash in on the stage antics bit. The string section, Kaminski, Mike Edwards and Hugh McDowell might have brought a rather sluggish audience to life if they had acted with the same enthusiasm on other numbers apart from Beethoven and Ma Ma Ma Belle.

Musically ELO are developing into a tight working unit progressing smoothly and it's healthy to see Jeff and his extraordinary group doing well and opening up a few eyes.

JOHN BEATTIE

Lynne told *New Musical Express* in March 1974; "Sure, I love a lot of classical music, but there's also a helluva lot that I don't like. I suppose I've got the same kinda taste as the average bloke in the street. You know — a little bit of Beethoven and Tchaikovsky, but I don't like none of this modern pseudo-intellectual stuff — the stuff that usually sounds like crashing cans. The last thing you could accuse ELO of being is pretentious. From the very start, we've carefully avoided the problem that some groups have of taking themselves too bloody serious — the ultra-cool far-out-man brigade. Yeah, we play some serious stuff — well, let's say: as serious as we want it to be. But we've always managed to offset that part of our programme with some harmless nonsense. That was the reason why we came up with 'Roll Over Beethoven' and 'In The Hall Of The Mountain King'. We weren't doing any rowdy rockers at the time and we thought it would be good fun to arrange them for our instrumentation as a bit of a laugh."

Recorded at London's De Lane Lea Studios between February and August, ELO's fourth album, *Eldorado*, was released in autumn 1974 in the UK on Warner Bros. Records and on United Artists Records in the US. It got to number sixteen in the US and to number seven in Canada.

Lynne said of the album; "I don't think the music was necessarily more commercial than *On The Third Day*. It was more accessible, probably, with much better tunes. Before *Eldorado*, I was, to some extent, working slightly against myself by not really letting myself go completely and doing songs that I think are great. I was holding back slightly and thinking 'maybe it's a bit dodgy', or whatever."

Not only did *Eldorado* achieve gold status in the US, but the first single released from it, 'Can't Get It Out Of My Head' (with 'Illusions In G Major' on the B-side), marked a significant milestone for the band by becoming their first top ten hit in the US when it got to number nine. *Record World* said of it; "Jeff Lynne and company brew up a brilliant batch of hook melody strains from the last decade of ballads into one fresh triumph."

Hilversum, Netherlands, 1974.
(Gijsbert Hanekroot / Alamy Stock Photo)

Electric Light Orchestra

Electric Light Orchestra, above, and the Edgar Winter Group, will be in concert Saturday at 8 p.m. at Henry Levitt Arena. Tickets are on sale at Argus Tapes and Records, Budget Tapes and Records, Sgt. Pepper's Parlor and the Central Agency for $5 in advance and $5.50 at the door.

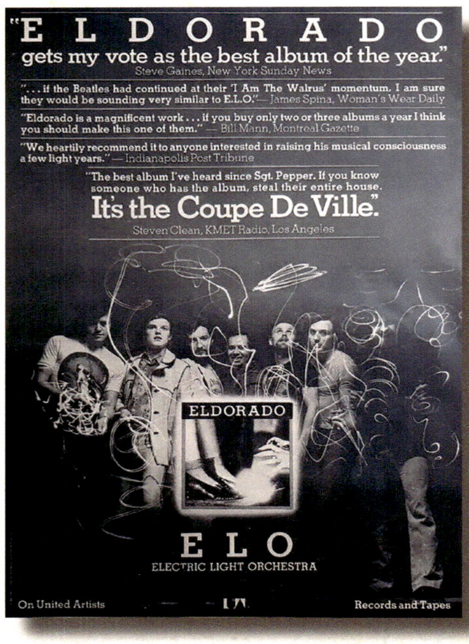

Eldorado was ELO's first concept album. Lynne had a well-defined storyline in mind before composing any of the music. The album's narrative centres on a character reminiscent of Walter Mitty, who embarks on journeys into fantastical realms through his dreams, seeking an escape from the monotony and disillusionment of his everyday life. In accordance with the album's theme, its cover, designed by John Kehe, features an image of Dorothy's ruby slippers from the 1939 movie, *The Wizard Of Oz*.

The inspiration for *Eldorado* emerged in response to Lynne's personal experiences. His father, a fan of classical music, had criticised ELO's repertoire, suggesting that the music lacked distinctive melodies. This feedback from his father motivated Lynne to craft an album that would not only feature captivating melodies, but also weave a compelling narrative.

Lynne said of his father; "His favourite composers were classical. He couldn't read or write music, but he used to be able to play Chopin on the piano with one finger. My dad didn't encourage me that much, but he bought me my first guitar for two pounds, so I had a good initiation, until my fingers bled. Then I got him to sign the papers on an electric Burns Sonic and a ten-watt amp."

With *Eldorado*, a notable shift in the band's approach occurred. For the first time, Lynne opted to bring an orchestra into the recording process, marking a departure from the earlier practice of having band members play strings on multi-tracked overdubbing. Louis Clark played a key role as a co-arranger alongside Lynne (and the band's keyboardist, Richard Tandy). Additionally, Clark conducted the orchestral sections.

Overall, *Eldorado* showcases a balance between orchestral and in-house string performances; although an orchestra was brought in, the band's three resident string players remained involved in the recording process. Their contributions are especially prominent on 'Boy Blue' and 'Laredo Tornado'.

September 1974.
(Pictorial Press Ltd / Alamy Stock Photo)

C LIGHT

September 1974.
(Pictorial Press Ltd / Alamy Stock Photo)

C LIGHT

Electric Light Orchestra Near Payoff

ROLLING STONE

SAN FRANCISCO – When WNCN, the New York classical station, changed its format to rock and its call letters to WQIV, it chose an ideal transition tune as a debut: the Chuck Berry classic, "Roll Over Beethoven." The choice was ideal for a second reason: The station used a version of the song by the Electric Light Orchestra, melding a rock oldie with one of the hottest new rock groups.

The group had a hit with "Roll Over Beethoven" last year, and while it is not representative of the range of ELO's musical ambitions, it conveniently furnished them with momentum. The plan then was to tour exhaustively in the U.S., and they're now into their fourth trek in 13 months.

And the payoff seems to be at hand: ELO's fourth album, "Eldorado," sold more than 250,000 units in its first month of release, receives heavy airplay (particularly on college stations) and bullets madly up the charts, while the current tour (their first to be properly coordinated with an album release) finds them packing 3,000-4,000-seat halls and getting a surprisingly effusive response from audiences that have come to see the headliner, Deep Purple.

ELO's evolution into a hitmaker wasn't easy. Jeff Lynne, cofounder and musical director, described it during the group's stopover in San Francisco. Nodding toward a sliding-glass door, through which would be seen an in-progress highrise looming uncomfortably close to his hotel room, he said, "It sounded like that sound out there." That sound was a clattering, whining chain saw, and Lynne said that was what the first incarnation of the ELO approximated. "Really bad sound. No tone at all. We only got a scraping noise or a really deep rumble."

They were aiming for the string- and keyboard-based rhythmic sound that they eventually found, but only after a lot of experimentation, and after Lynne inherited control of the cacophony from the Move (a group he, Roy Wood and ELO's drummer, Bev Bevan, had founded). The Move was successful in England, but never attained the quality that Lynne and Wood had envisioned.

The setting was Birmingham, England, where the music scene had a sophisticated and decidedly eccentric flavor – the emphasis was on vocal harmonies (the Beach Boys and the Four Seasons were the big heroes) and, according to Bevan, Indonesian rhythms managed to find their way to the city, too.

The gnomish Wood, now the painted witch doctor of Wizzard, has explained the process that led to the ELO: "In the early Move days I was a big fan of the Beatles, especially 'I Am the Walrus' and 'Strawberry Fields' and things like that, with the George Martin string sound on them . . . And I thought, wouldn't it be great if you could represent this onstage properly with your own band? . . . Like instead of having a guitarist, have a cello player or a French horn player, and not have to use sessionmen."

Wood cited songwriting as Lynne's chief contribution, but Bevan and Lynne say that Lynne had more to do with the basic concept than Wood lets on.

The threesome disbanded the Move and recorded an ELO album by themselves (Wood handling most of the strings), and then collected the appropriate musicians, rehearsed for months, and hit the road to find instant disaster.

"We did maybe 20 dates," Bevan said in Los Angeles this fall, "and it never sounded any good. It sounded terrible in fact. There were too many musicians onstage, and Roy would change instruments every number, so there were, like, five-minute gaps between numbers. He used to wear these old black glasses that you couldn't possibly see through, and every night he used to fall over stuff, crashing to the floor. It must have been really boring to watch."

Wood finally made his inevitable departure, and it was up to Lynne to sort out the players and disastrous noise. "We suffered along like that for about three months," he said, "and then somebody said something about Barcus-Berry pickups, and we tried one on the cello and it was fabulous. Suddenly it sounded good, like real strings. We got that sounding good, with the Moog, so suddenly from the terrible whistling, banging sort of noises we used to create, came all these lovely, rich string bands. In about a week we changed the sound of the group to more or less the sound we've got now."

Mik Kaminski and Hugh McDowall trade string for string during the Electric Light Orchestra's performance at the Cow Palace in San Francisco.

Lynne has the reliable, assured air of a veteran, and while his wooly growth of hair and beard and his concealing sunglasses minimize facial expression and give him an almost forbidding aura, he's an affable, if not especially self-revealing, sort. He writes all of ELO's material, arranges it, produces the records and establishes the ideals that the group must meet. But he downplays his role as leader, insisting that ELO be seen as a group, not an interchangeable bunch of musicians mechanically executing his ideas.

"It's very much a group thing onstage," he maintains. "It's in the studio where I take control, 'cause I'm contracted to write all the stuff by my publishing deal, which I can't possibly get out of. Onstage, we probably do half my songs and half standards that we've redone."

Lynne, on guitar and most of the vocals, could hardly hope to dominate the controlled chaos that ELO unleashes in performance. The imposing Bevan, who plays soccer in his spare time and looks it, brings both power and delicacy to the drumming, playing with the effortless ease of an expert chef gracefully flipping crepes into the air. Lynne, Bevan, Kelly Groucutt (bass) and Richard Tandy (keyboards) maintain a low profile onstage, leaving cellists Hugh McDowall and Mike Edwards and violinist Mik Kaminski in charge of the mayhem.

The group is studious enough when they execute their more formal pieces, but they know what a rock & roll show is and are willing to milk the humorous side of the meeting of cello and electric guitar.

"Great Balls of Fire" and "Roll Over Beethoven" (and this is really where they pick up the Deep Purple crowd) become a searing sonic backdrop for a series of acrobatics, and pile into an overkill crescendo that ends only when Edwards' cello literally explodes in his hand.

Tandy, an old Birmingham buddy, was the first recruit to ELO's current lineup. "Richard," Lynne said, "is one of the most important members of the group, 'cause he's got so much to do. He does an incredible amount of work onstage. He's got a mellotron, Moog and piano, and he has to keep them all going at once. Millions of pedals and knobs. In the studio he's my right hand. He plays all the instruments I want to put on that I can't play, so he always comes into the studio more than anybody else."

Mike Edwards looks like a Walt Disney dwarf and was snatched from the Royal Academy of Music, where he taught cello. Bevan calls Hugh McDowall "the first rock & roll star cellist. He's got a great image and he looks good onstage. Like a pop idol, but with a cello. There's never been one of those before."

Friday, December 6, 1974 Sentinel Star 11–E

ELO head out

ELO are following up their current Stateside success with a single, I Can't Get It Out Of My Head, released on February 28. The cut is taken from their Eldorado album which has already gone gold in America.

After their British tour the band go to Europe for dates in Germany, Scandinavia, Spain, Yugoslavia, Austria, Switzerland, Holland and Belgium. They then tour Australia and return to America in the Autumn.

Whilst the recording of *Eldorado* was still in progress, Mike de Albuquerque decided to leave ELO. His departure was motivated by a desire to spend more time with his family. Consequently, much of the bass on the album was handled by Lynne.

When an edited version of 'Boy Blue' (with 'Eldorado' on the B-side) was released as a single in the US, it didn't garner commercial success — much like the release of *Eldorado* in ELO's home country of the UK! Still though, *Cash Box* considered; "a big symphonic sound surrounds and cushions a driving rock beat on this excellently-produced Jeff Lynne track." *Record World* called the song "just familiar enough on the first listen," adding, "this azure lad brings on visions of 'Hang On Sloopy', then heads out on its own."

Rolling Stone said of *Eldorado*: "Here Lynne shines — the eight individual tracks represent the strongest, most varied set yet recorded by ELO. 'Can't Get It Out Of My Head' is an immediate favourite, vaguely suggestive of The Kinks, with a lush, irresistibly pretty melody. Other standouts include 'Illusions In G Major', a skilful, power-packed fifties-style rocker with intriguing lyrics; 'Poor Boy', a robber ballad cleverly employing an uncanny Bob Dylan *John Wesley Harding* era sound-alike vocal. 'Mister Kingdom' pleasantly evokes The Beatles' 'Across The Universe'; 'Boy Blue' is an enjoyable, extremely simple rock number; and 'Eldorado', though embarrassingly rotund in spots, is a tuneful Bee Gees-like ballad. As a concept album, *Eldorado* is lyrically effective and thankfully not overbearing. The symphonic aspects sometimes get out of hand, but generally work well enough. And as for the rest, *Eldorado* is the most successful Electric Light Orchestra album to date."

Lynne told *Melody Maker*; "Obviously, I'm influenced by The Beatles, because The Beatles of '68 and '69 was the sound I have always liked. That's obviously been a big influence on the way I've looked at songwriting. If you're going to be influenced, you might as well be influenced by the best stuff."

ELO, Deep Purple Create Very Good Sounds, Sights

By MIKE DIANA

With the sad state the economy's in it was no wonder Norfolk Scope was only half full for an evening with Deep Purple, Electric Light Orchestra (ELO) and Elf.

The Tuesday night concert was the last stop on the American tour and England's ELO and Purple warned the audience that the evening was going to be one of those "anything goes" happenings with good music and good times for all. And, at least for ELO, it was.

The Electric Light Orchestra incorporates two cellos, a viola and a mellotron (taped instrument sounds, such as flute, violin and cello with chords being formed through keyboard) along with the usual guitar, bass and drums into their material, lending, at times, a symphonia to otherwise standard rock fare.

From the moment the lights came up and the music started (a bit too loud at first) ELO took command of the arena with a set that gradually built in energy and intensity. And when the lights went down after the encore the auditorium was alive and buzzing with excitement. ELO stole the show.

Maybe the boys were just excited to be going home for Christmas, or overjoyed to have finished another exhausting tour, but whatever it was they were loose and having a ball on stage.

Their set consisted of material from the early ELO albums and cuts from the new "Eldorado" Lp. The band handled the Beatle's "Day Tripper" along with rockers like "Roll Over Beethoven" (laced with Ludwig's fifth symphony) and the Jerry Lee Lewis hit, "Great Balls of Fire" with comparitive ease. Also heard were "Flight of the Bumble Bee" (a segment of a spotlighted cello solo) and a strong rendition of "In the Hall of the Mountain King."

Wacky things began to happen during the much-called-for encore. One of the cellists was tapped on the shoulder and hit in the face with a shaving cream pie. A member of the ELO stage crew just let him have it. (He the cellist) was trying to play the entire time this was going on. It appeared to be entirely unrehearsed. He couldn't have faked the shocked and well-foamed expression on his face.

After the pie and still during the encore Bev Bevan, drummer for the group, had his entire set stolen. That's right...while he was playing. Another member of the ELO road crew walked out on stage during the encore number and began disasembling Bevan's kit. Then one by one other crew members appeared and began carrying off all of his drums, cymbals and standds. Bevan was left with his sticks and his snare drum with which he tried to continue the number while looking about the stage for help. Later the snare was taken off stage and he ran after the thief to retrieve it. The other band members were finding it difficult to play through their laughter. One cellist wound up whanging his cello (whanging?) like Elvis wangs his guitar...hip gyrations included. The other, who was dressed like a gentleman from the time of Queen Victoria, ended the night climbing to the top of the amplifiers, playing all the way up.

The music and the antics, including an exploding cello, combined to make seeing the Electric Light Orchestra worth the price of admission.

Deep Purple had a big job in trying to surpass their support act and though they tried their best they were hard pressed to match up.

The group, led by guitarist Richard Blackmore, played with enough energy and volume to cause half of Norfolk to blackout...and most of the audience to follow suit.

Purple's first number was the title track from the "Burn" album, released earlier this year, and, because of the volume, left ears flapping in the sonic breeze. With one's fingers in one's ears you were able to cut through the distortion and reverberation and actually hear the music through the noise.

The songs were called by the two new members of the group, lead vocalist is Coverdale and bassist, vocalist Hughes.

Coverdale an unknown, answered an add and was picked out of an audition where some name people were also trying out. When asked how becoming a rock star had changed his life Coverdale said that he was going to buy the boutique he used to work in.

Hughes has been around for a while playing bass, writing and singing for Trapeze, a three piece powerhouse of music.

Hughes and Coverdale are impressive and have improved the vocal work for Deep Purple a hundred fold. Hughes bass playing adds a good bit of raunchy funk to a group that used to do strong flowing music.

I must admit, though I was shriveled and driven to a headache by the unrelenting volume, Purple's set was strong and well performed.

The Electric Light Orchestra, English rock group, comes to the Mary E. Sawyer Auditorium at 7:30 p.m. Thursday, Apr 18, in a show that also stars the REO Speedwagon.

THE CINCINNATI ENQUIRER Tuesday, December 3, 1974

Garden Walls Nearly Fall To Deep Purple Jackhammer

By ROBERT UTH
Enquirer Contributor

Remember this old lyric? "When the deep purple falls over sleepy garden walls, and the stars begin to twinkle in the blue."

Well, sometimes old lyrics come true, as proved by the British rock group Deep Purple, Sunday night at the Cincinnati Gardens.

ALMOST TRUE. The group didn't fall over the Garden's walls, but instead tried to crumble the structure with high- decibel sound. And the stars, instead of twinkling in the blue, roared amid a panoply of colored lights and fog makers.

But all that came last. Two groups preceded this electronic onslaught.

Having arrived near the end of the first group's opening number, I found it necessary to ask a fan sitting next to me if she knew the name of the group. She just shrugged as if it didn't matter. After the group concluded their performance, I decided she was right. (**Editor's Note:** The group was "Elf.")

NEXT, an exciting performance from the Electric Light Orchestra. Though formerly a sleeper on the popular charts, the ELO has recently gained a strong following with two top singles: "Raining All Over the World," and "Eldorado."

Many spectators were expecting normal rock concert fare—garbage mixed with hits. But this was not the case. Mixing versatile musicianship with crowd-pleasing theatricality, the ELO proved themselves both a first-rate recording and performing ensemble.

Working in front of a large light sculpture resembling an incandescent light bulb, the group members whirled and gyrated, spicing all this motion with an unusual habit of playing their instruments upside down.

Seen from the rear, this unique setting looked like a large mass of people worshiping a light bulb.

And why not? Electricity is the main ingredient in the ELO's sound —so much so that the stage becomes a giant high-fi set, rather than a platform for performers.

BUT ALL this sophisticated and synthesized instrumentation created a problem for vocalists. In contrast to any synthesized instrument, the human voice always sounds like an anachronism. Of course, any vocalist can run his voice through a synthesizer, but the result is anything but human.

In spite of vocal problems, it was obvious that most of the personnel in the ELO had undergone classical training. Take for example Hugh McDowell's rendition of "Flight of the Bumble Bee" on synthesized, upside down cello. And for an encore, what could be more appropriate than Beethoven's "Fifth Symphony," cleverly folded into Chuck Berry's "Roll Over Beethoven."

In preparation for Deep Purple's appearance, stage technicians performed the curious concert phenomenon known as "stacking." This involves the construction of a wall of about 25 speakers, each addition increasing anticipation for what is billed as "the loudest show in rock."

In this case, the stacking proved somewhat anticlimactic as Deep Purple's concert had about as much musical substance as a jackhammer. In fact, one couldn't help but wonder why Deep Purple wasn't the warm-up group for the Electric Light Orchestra.

Arrangements were essentially monotonous, and instrumentation seldom got beyond the riff or the short run.

MIDWAY through their performance, the group presented that strange innovation of British hard rockers—aimless blues. When lead singer Ian Gillan stood in front of the audience and wailed, "I've been mistreated," it seemed as if he was using the crowd as the object of his vengeance.

Theatricality mitigated some of the cacophony, but it was difficult not to imagine Gillan reworking his lead vocals in "Jesus Christ Superstar" as he stood moaning within billowing clouds of artificial fog.

Of course, hits were mixed with garbage, and the group's rendition of "Smoke On the Water" drew pleased fans up to and onto the stage.

In spite of the unpleasant, reverbrating sound, one good thing came out of the Deep Purple concert—the Electric Light Orchestra.

Over November and December 1974, ELO furthered their reputation in America when they toured as support to Deep Purple, often getting better reviews than the headliners. Despite having been announced as the biggest selling US album act of 1973, by this stage in their tenure, many reviewers saw Deep Purple as being too long in the tooth. For example, Robert Uth writing for the *Cincinnati Enquirer* said; "One couldn't help but wonder why Deep Purple wasn't the warm-up group for Electric Light Orchestra." Uth completed his review of Deep Purple by saying, "in spite of the unpleasant reverberating sound, one good thing came out of the Deep Purple concert — the Electric Light Orchestra."

Rolling Stone said; "*Eldorado* sold more than 250,000 in its first month of release, receives heavy airplay (particularly on college stations) and bullets madly up the charts, while the current tour (their first to be properly co-ordinated with an album release) finds them packing three-thousand to four-thousand–seat halls and getting a surprisingly effusive response from audiences that have come to see the headliner, Deep Purple."

During the tour, Hugh McDowell even gave Deep Purple's Ritchie Blackmore some cello lessons!

Around this period, ELO was becoming more visual on stage. Keen to appear more exciting, the string section devised several visual gags. Hugh McDowell threw his cello in the air, and Mike Edwards blew his up. Edwards' first party piece involved miming playing *The Dying Swan* while rolling an orange down the neck of his cello. From there, he graduated to explosives.

"I didn't really fancy it, but they had this thing built," Edwards explained. "Hugh would be playing this piece and I would be miming to it on this cello. At a key moment, he pressed a button with his foot and the cello fell apart in a puff of smoke, leaving him "playing" a mess of wood and strings. Then we'd put it back together for the next day."

Lynne, Gale and Groucett around 1975. Melvyn Gale: "My parents had no real idea what I was doing. They thought I was part of a backing orchestra for the group. It was only at the charity Wembley show in 1978 that they suddenly twigged. I arranged for a limo to collect them from Beckenham and take them up and back and I introduced my mum to Tony Curtis (she was a big fan of his), then it sank in." (Interviewed by Martin Kinch, 2009)
(Laurens van Hooten / Pictorial Press Ltd / Alamy Stock Photo)

SOUNDS OF TODAY

Eldorado looms for Jeff Lynne

JEFF LYNNE seems to have found his own personal Eldorado with the new Electric Light Orchestra album.

After three years of trying, this famous son of Birmingham and long suffering Blues supporter has achieved his musical aim.

In "Eldorado" (Warner Brothers), the Electric Light Orchestra have married a suite of strong, commercial, listenable pop songs into an integrated symphonic structure.

And I have a hunch that E.L.O.'s Birmingham concert next Monday — at which "Eldorado" is bound to be featured—will be a massive triumph.

JEFF LYNNE . . . going great with E.L.O.

Contrast

On the surface, it is the same mixture as its predecessor, the excellent "On the Third Day."

Jeff's echo-charged rasping tones, which bring John Lennon to mind on slower numbers, contrast sharply with the luscious cellos and violins that dominate the arrangements.

And Bev Bevan — Jeff's fellow refugee from the Move —holds it all together with some beautifully solid drumming.

The whole of side one is com posed of memorable pop tunes.

"Boy Blue" sees Jeff using moog synthesiser to simulate brass backing—and features arresting pauses which break up the song before it crashes on.

"Laredo Tornado" and "Poor Boy" feature the string section at its lushest and richest — while remaining simple direct tunes.

But "Can't Get It Out of My Head" is the real clincher —a plaintive Lennonish slow tune with a chorus that hits you first time round.

Witty

The second side offers some variety—"Painted Lady" has a more bluesy feel and relies on piano rather than string backing.

And the misleadingly titled "Illusions in G Major" is nothing but good old rock and roll, with nice witty lyrics. It could almost have been written by Chuck Berry.

The lyrics, which are sustained throughout all the songs, are about a dreamer travelling and searching for the key to the eternal dream.

But like some pop "symphonies" I could mention, it is never ponderous, pretentious, or boring.

Jeff ensures that the songs are rooted in straightforward pop, and his presence guarantees a down to earth feeling.

Singles

It's strange that he and the ELO are revered in America, where the album and "Can't Get It Out of My Head" are in the respective Top 30s.

But here they're vastly underrated, being regarded as a single band only.

Despite this, ELO, totally original, are attempting things that few other bands are doing.

I hope the Town Hall is packed next weeek for the finest band Birmingham has exported to the world.

DAVID GRITTEN

THE "LIGHT" IS ON AT PEACHES

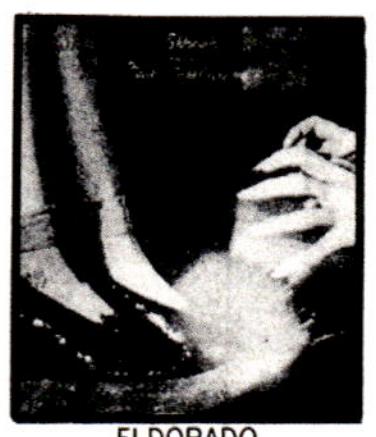

ELDORADO
A Symphony by the Electric Light Orchestra

"ON THE THIRD DAY"
Electric Light Orchestra

ELECTRIC LIGHT ORCHESTRA II

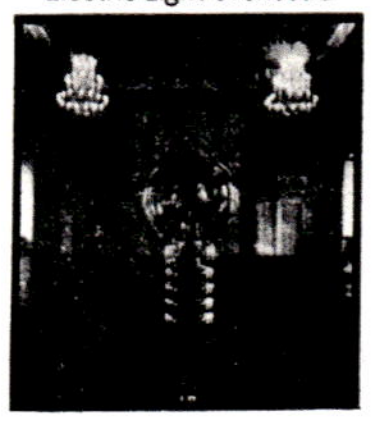

THE ELECTRIC LIGHT ORCHESTRA

Peaches
RECORDS & TAPES
2282 Peachtree Road 352-1704

Soon though, Edwards seemed to tire of the on-stage antics. After *Eldorado* was released, several line-up changes occurred. Kelly Groucutt was brought in as the new bassist, and in early 1975, Melvyn Gale took over from Mike Edwards as the cellist. These adjustments contributed to a more stable line-up as ELO transitioned towards a notably more accessible sound.

By this point, the band had established a strong presence in the US. A star attraction on the stadium and arena circuit, their popularity was further underscored by appearances on *The Midnight Special*.

ELO's fifth album, *Face The Music* was released in autumn 1975 — on Don Arden's Jet Records in the UK and on United Artists Records in the US. The album's sound moved away from the grand-scale classical orchestration of *Eldorado*. Instead, the band embraced a more radio-friendly pop rock approach whilst still featuring string sections in their songs. This new musical direction proved to be a successful pivot for the group. As well as getting to number eight in the US, *Face The Music* earned the distinction of becoming the first ELO album to achieve platinum status there, a clear testament to its commercial impact.

After completing the European segment of the Eldorado tour, ELO recorded *Face The Music* at Musicland Studios in Munich, Germany. Interestingly, the recommendation to use Musicland Studios came from Deep Purple, with whom ELO had frequently shared the stage during their initial North American leg of the Eldorado tour. With Lynne holding the facilities in high regard and considering his good working rapport with sound engineer Reinhold Mack, Musicland Studios would go on to become a significant location for the recording of several of ELO's future albums.

Strings all a-rocking

SINCE the formation of the Electric Light Orchestra (above) in 1972 founder member Jeff Lynne has worked towards his original concept of the fusion of rock band and orchestra.

Now he's achieved his aim and successfully combined a classical style with their original rock music on their fourth album, Eldorado. To create the sound, the seven-man group combined with a 30-piece string orchestra, a 10-piece brass section and a choir of 20.

Eldorado is the story of one man's quest for a mythological city on a hill, and every track reflects one of his dreams. The album is already among the top sellers in America, where the Electric Light Orchestra have won a huge following on tours.

They're back in Britain now after an absence of nearly 10 months and will present a live interpretation of some of the new album tracks in their concert at Birmingham Town Hall on Monday.

A new band, Chopyn, joins the Electric Light Orchestra on the tour. The brainchild and founder of Chopyn is Ann Odell, who is possibly best known as the keyboard player for Blue Mink. She's been in the business, playing session music for several years, but she found it frustrating. She wanted a band that could go on the road and could let themselves go and enjoy playing. The result was Chopyn, formed this year.

Nev Victoria
ROBIN DENSELOW

Electric Light Orchestra

THE ELECTRIC Light Orchestra—the rather more arty spin-off to that delightfully lightweight Sixties group, The Move — are so successful in America these days that a London concert is something of a rarity for them. Along with bands like Renaissance (again, far more popular in the States than here), and the late Moody Blues, the ELO have realised the growing audience for slickly performed ballads, dressed up with a wall of sound. The appeal is to the more middle-of-the-road, "easy listening" audience, as well as rock audiences.

At this concert they managed to transcend the "arty muzac" category—but only just—by throwing in the occasional burst of originality or excellent playing into what was essentially an extremely safe, if professional, performance. Their line-up was interesting: two electric cellos and an electric violin alongside the conventional guitar, bass and drums, but the strings were rarely allowed to dominate the music in any interesting way.

Most of the time they simply provided lush backings to Jeff Lynne's ballads; and the sound they produced was not that different to that which one mellatron might have provided. The technical expertise of the cellists and violinists was shown in their solo spots and the occasional classically influenced flourishes they were allowed (as at the start of Eldorado), but there was little interesting interplay between them and Lynne's guitar. By the end—when everyone was bashing out the usual rockriffs, the ELO sounded like just another goodish band.

Colston Hall Bristol

ADVANCE BOOKINGS, phone 291768, or LEWIS'S TRAVEL BUREAU or BLACKBOY RECORDS for all performances.

TONIGHT at 7.30
SLOVAK CHAMBER ORCHESTRA
Brandenburg Concerto No. 3 ... Bach
Suite Abdalazer ... Purcell
Serenade for Strings ... Suchon
The Four Seasons ... Vivaldi
Director and Soloist:
BOHDAN WARCHAL
£1.25, £1, 75p, 55p, 30p

TOMORROW at 7.45
Superstar WRESTLING
Jon Guil Don v. Bobby Barnes
Clive Myers v. Vic Faulkner
Bert Royal v. Mick McManus
Neil Sands v. Steve Viedor
Robby Baron v. Bob Kirkwood
85p, 70p, 55p, 45p, 30p

SATURDAY, FEB. 15, at 7.30
MASSED BANDS CONCERT
STANSHAWE (Bristol) BAND
BRIGHOUSE AND RASTRICK BAND
Guest Conductor:
JAMES SCOTT
75p 65p, 50p, 40p

MONDAY, FEB. 17, at 7.30
Derek Block presents
ELECTRIC LIGHT ORCHESTRA
with CHOPYN
£1.25, £1, 75p

TUESDAY, FEB. 18, at 7.30
Chrysalis presents
ROBIN TROWER
IN CONCERT
with the
MANDALA BAND
90p, 75p, 60p

WEDNESDAY, FEB. 19, at 7.30
Bournemouth Symphony Orchestra
Symphony No. 40 ... Mozart
Symphonic Poem MacBeth ... Richard Strauss
Symphony No. [illegible] ... Dvorak
JOHN PRITCHARD
£1.50, £1.30, £1, 75p, 50p, 40p

FRIDAY, FEB. 21, at 7.30
GILBERT & SULLIVAN FOR ALL
with
Angela Jenkins, Jean Temperley
Thomas Round, Donald Adams
and John Cartier
GILBERT & SULLIVAN SOCIETY
BRISTOL SAVOY OPERATIC
BRISTOL CATHOLIC PLAYERS
Musical Director:
CLIVE TIMMS
£1, 80p, 60p, 40p

SATURDAY, FEB. 22, at 7.30
John Smith Entertainments
THE KIKI DEE BAND
IN CONCERT
with Special Guests:
SAILOR
All seats bookable, £1

SUNDAY, FEB. 23, at 7.30
Peter Bowyer presents
THE AL STEWART BAND
with
BRINSLEY SCHWARZ
£1.25, £1, 75p

MONDAY, FEB. 24, at 7.30
World Wide Entertainments presents
MARTIAL ARTS
LIVE ON STAGE
JUDO, KARATE, KUNG FU
AIKIDO, KENDO, SELF-DEFENCE
NUNCHAKUS DISPLAY, STICK FIGHTING, LIVE SAMURAI SWORD FIGHTING
£1, 80p, 60p

WEDNESDAY, FEB. 26, at 7.30
BRISTOL SINFONIA
SIDNEY SAGER
Concerto Grosso Op. [illegible] ... Corelli
Clarinet Concerto ... Mozart
Fantasia on a theme of Corelli ... Tippett
Symphony No. [illegible] ... Schubert
ANGELA MALSBURY
£1.25, £1, 75p, 55p, 30p

WVUD & PANTHER PRODUCTIONS PRESENTS
ELECTRIC LIGHT ORCHESTRA
with special guest
PAVLOV'S DOG
Sunday, June 29, 8:00 P.M.
DAYTON HARA ARENA
Tickets, $5.00 Advance, 6.00 Day of Show
Tickets on sale all TICKTRON outlets, Cincinnati
Hamilton, Middletown. Phone 278-4776.

As the band's only songwriter, Lynne sought to create music that would not only be memorable but would serve as a departure from the progressive rock style found on ELO's initial three albums and the largely symphonic sound of *Eldorado*. To achieve this new musical landscape, several measures were implemented to ensure a more intricate, yet satisfying, sound. These measures included the addition of female backing vocalists — Ellie Greenwich, Susan Collins, Nancy O'Neill, and Margaret Raymond. Furthermore, a choir was incorporated into the arrangements. Additionally, the band's string trio — consisting of Mik Kaminski, Hugh McDowell, and Melvyn Gale — played a more integrated role in the recordings. They were mixed into the ensemble of a thirty-piece string section, and their contributions extended to performing solos. This innovative approach added a new dimension to the band's sound, placing emphasis on both complexity and listening pleasure.

"A lot of the material we do is two-sided," Lynne said at the time. "There's a typically classical side to our songs as well as a typically rock side. With this band, it's gotten to the point where it's actually hard to separate the classical and rock sounds. The sound is fusing together and the band's musical influences are crossing over and mixing."

"The effective fusing of these sounds is the whole idea behind the band," added Bevan. "What we're doing has never been done before. People like Deep Purple and Procol Harum have worked with symphony orchestras, but it's always been basically two separate units working at different times. Ours is a mixture of both sounds."

At De Lane Lea Studios in London, the orchestra was recorded separately from the band's initial recording sessions. This approach allowed for meticulous attention to detail and contributed to the rich and complex orchestral elements in the album's music.

Hugh McDowell on tour in the States in 1975.
(Jeffrey Mayer / Pictorial Press Ltd / Alamy Stock Photo)

Jeff Lynne and his friends

Rock and orchestra

By RICK ATKINSON
Rock Critic

For years people have been dabbling with the concept of a fusion of rock music and orchestral instruments, but none of them has ever matched the musical and financial success of the Electric Light Orchestra. Fans of Jeff Lynne and his rock-classical cohorts can now celebrate the release of the group's fifth album, "Face the Music."

The Electric Light Orchestra (known to fans as ELO) had its beginnings in a Birmingham (England)-based British group called The Move. In 1970, after a four-year history of hit singles, Move mainstays Roy Wood and Bev. Bevan invited a Birmingham guitarist named Jeff Lynne to join their recently depleted ranks. Lynne had been offered the job several times before, but had always refused. To induce Lynne to join, Wood described plans for the group's future: a new line-up with its own self-contained string section. Lynne liked the idea, and The Move became a trio.

The hardest part of the transition from The Move to the Electric Light Orchestra was finding a record label. Although the musicians could point with pride to a string of hit records, record company people were afraid of the new idea. When the group finally signed a contract, it was with a stipulation they didn't really like: The Move had to continue, at least in the studio, until ELO was a proven success. Wood, Lynne, and Bevan suddenly found themselves in two groups at the same time.

The first album by ELO, "No Answer," was finally released in mid-1972. The album is more The Move than ELO. There were just Wood, Lynne, and Bevan with one or two extra friends playing a lot of different instruments. The groundwork was there, but the concept was still unrealized.

Between "No Answer" and the recording of the second album, "ELO II," friction developed between Lynne and Wood: Despite the fact that both shared the work equally, the better-known Wood was seen by many as the group leader. The question was resolved when Wood left to form his own group, leaving Lynne and Bevan to run ELO.

'Roll over Beethoven'

Lynne and Bevan lost no time beefing up the group's roster and recording the second ELO album. They were an immediate success, largely due to the success of a single called "Roll Over Beethoven." The group took the old Chuck Berry song and gave it new life; a medley of the rock tune and snatches from Beethoven's work, with the string section handling the classical music very adeptly. It was a corny gimmick, but it met with startling success.

A third album, "On the Third Day," brought the band international fame. They finally toured this country as a headline act, playing in such prestigious halls as New York's Philharmonic Hall (now Avery Fischer Hall).

"Eldorado," the band's fourth album, brought still greater fame, and was the band's first gold album, signifying a million dollars in album sales. A single from the album, "Can't Get It Out of My Head," lingered on the charts for weeks.

This fifth album, "Face the Music," should easily follow in the golden tracks of "Eldorado." Some personnel changes (Kelly Groucutt replacing Michael De Albuquerque on bass; Melvyn Gale replacing Michael Edwards on cello) have tightened up the band's sound greatly, and the new set of Lynne compositions easily equal those on the previous album.

Like "Eldorado," "Face the Music" is a concept album. It starts with a fascinating instrumental piece called "Fire on High" which serves as an introduction, much as "Eldorado Overture" did on the previous album. This new track, however, seems to be almost a conscious effort to show just how much ELO can do with its lineup. The guitar and the string section switch the song's lead back and forth in a constant musical tug-of-war; the group is superb on either level.

The only real instrumental change on this album is the noticeable increase in the amount of work Richard Tandy is contributing. His use of the synthesizer for additional musical texture is much more prominent here than on previous albums.

With outstanding tracks such as "Waterfall," "Down Home Town," and "Nightrider," there can be little doubt that the Electric Light Orchestra is in for a lot of success with "Face the Music."

HOT FLASHES: The new Stanley Clarke album, "Journey to Love," features Jeff Beck, John McLaughlin, Lenny White, and George Duke as guest artists . . . The new American tour by The Who is being done in two parts. Part One will run from Nov. 20 through Dec. 15, covering 20 concerts in 19 cities.

No New York date has been announced for the first part of the tour, with the closest show to here being in Philadelphia on Dec. 15. Dates for the second part of the tour will be announced within the next three weeks . . . The new album by Roxy Music will be called "Siren," and features a single called "Love Is the Drug" . . . "Beginnings," the solo album by Yes guitarist Steve Howe, is now scheduled for release before Thanksgiving . . . Sire Records has an album called "The History of British Rock Volume Three" in the works . . . New albums by Led Zeppelin and The Rolling Stones are in the works, but neither will be out before the beginning of next year . . . Guitarist Roy Buchanan is in Electric Lady Studios recording his debut album for Atlantic Records. Arif Mardin will be the producer of the as-yet-untitled work.

Moody sound given a touch of John Lennon

By ROME SCOTT

Electric Light Orchestra Face the Music (United Artists Records)

Clinking and moaning, helter skelter pieces of orchestrated strings open the album with Hell in Heaven. "Fire on High" fashions images of a satanic orchestra tuning up to back the vocals of an angelic choir.

The Electric Light Orchestra has been remarkably silent since its radio hit "I Can't Get Her Out of My head," but with that single the group established its Moody Blues orchestration backing vocals characteristic of post-Beatles John Lennon.

Review

The band's sound is heavily symphonic with a violin and two cellos weaving their sensitive moodiness among strains of gutless synthesizer tones.

Guitarist Jeff Lynne's lead vocals bristle with the rough tenor John Lennon has used since leaving the Beatles to plant his voice so inextricably among the lush, smooth flow of strings and carefully arranged guitar.

And the ponderously heavy, black colorations of the strings are carried on a beat that moves too quickly, with too much life, bog down the sound.

The Electric Light Orchestra has done for classical rock what Chicago has done for big band rock.

The strings aren't used to fill in the holes or added as an afterthought, but are an essential part of the whole.

As with Chicago, which gave brass more than a background responsibility, Electric Light Orchestra's strings play in a position of prominence.

The concept works whether it is to create a breathlessly light whirlwind of notes or to form a sound so solid you felt as if you could hold it in your hands.

The music is grand with big sound on songs such as "Poker" and it's earthy as on "Down Home Town."

Never is the music self-conscious. Even during the full vocal harmonies of Lynne, drummer Bev Bevan and bass guitarist Kelly Groucutt, the instrumentals are full, but not domineering.

The vocals, however, aren't lifted out of the sound to block the subtle counter-melodies of the instruments.

(Pictorial Press Ltd / Alamy Stock Photo)

1975.
(Jeffrey Mayer / Pictorial Press Ltd / Alamy Stock Photo)

Kelly Groucett, who replaced Mike de Albuquerque for the tour in support of *Eldorado*. Groucett was more than just a bass player and contributed lead vocals on some tracks.
(Pictorial Press Ltd / Alamy Stock Photo)

1976.
(Pictorial Press Ltd / Alamy Stock Photo)

moog

POP: Gerald Radcliffe

Classical concoction

"Face the Music" — Electric Light Orchestra (JETLP 11)

OVERCOME, if you can, your initial distaste for (or, if you've a funny sense of humour, your amusement over) the sleeve of the latest ELO offering, showing on the front an electric chair under a haze of smoke and on the back the lads themselves in jaundiced hue and with the same horrible bulging eyeballs effect used to such lousy effect on a Hollies album of a couple of years back.

Inside things are in much better taste — and very tasty too. It could almost have been re-titled: "ELO's Tribute to Paul Macca and The Other Three" there's so much of a Wings/-Beatles sound shining through Jeff Lynne's beautiful melodies.

ELO being the Electric Light Orchestra, however, there's a deeper and richer feeling about the eight tracks included than even McCartney could manage. The violin and 'cellos of Mik Kaminsky, Hugh McDowall and Melvyn Gale are now blending superbly into the rather over-blown (but none the worse for it) rock-classics intentions of the outfit.

The outstanding track, of course, has to be the one that's already confirmed their immense stature in the States and looks set to get them back in the British charts, "Evil Woman," as melodic a rocker as ever Wings or even the Eagles could produce.

Even when they go in for "overkill" — as on the opening number, "Fire On High," with its poor imitation of the Huddersfield Choral Society's Hallelujah Chorus and some epic string sounds — at least they make it harmoniously and entertaingly pretentious.

The lyrics are not always very strong either; but with ELO that hardly matters. It's the overall sound that counts — and it adds up to very good effect on "Face The Music": full-bodied, flowing, rhythmic and rocking, yet maintaining an "old-fashioned" classical approach which manages to fill a room with moody sounds even when the volume's turned down low.

Perhaps Lancaster and Lumley should have given their "Peter And The Wolf" score to ELO. Working as a group — and with more respect for classical sounds — I'm sure they could have hung the work together better than the "various artists."

And one final point about that distasteful sleeve; intentional or not, did they really have to credit the art work to John Kehe and Mick Haggerty under the heading "Design and Execution"?"

■ ■ ■

TOP TEN

1 Glass of Champagne — Sailor
2 Mama Mia — Abba
3 Bohemian Rhapsody — Queen
4 Wide Eyed And Legless — Andy Fairweather Low
5 Art For Art's Sake — 10cc
6 Itchycoo Park — Small Faces
7 In Dulce Jubilo — Mike Oldfield
8 Golden Years — David Bowie
9 Trail Of The Lonesome Pine — Laurel and Hardy
10 Let's Twist Again — Chubby Checker

List compiled from information supplied by Boots, Victoria Lane; Smiths, Shambles; Woods, New Street; Woolworths, New Street and Menzies, New Street.

String along with ELO

ELO: all action

ELO/New Victoria, London

THE EASY way for a group to add strings to their sound these days is to use a synthesiser. The hard way is to use two cello players and violinist.

ELO have been doing it the hard way for years and it seems more satisfying (providing you can get the balance right), and especially when the cello player decides he is going to play it behind his head.

As any music master will tell you, the cello is not meant for playing rock on, but Hugh McDowell broke all the rules knocking out a 12-bar riff, but saved himself from disgrace by neatly turning it into the 'Flight Of The Bumble Bee'.

Jeff Lynne was in fine form, as was Bev Bevan, surrounded by all manner of percussion and unlike many drummers actually using them all.

They went back through most of their past achievements and an all action finale was ensured by doing 'Roll Over Beethoven', which might have been aptly written just for them.

The number enabled them to pull out all the stops, with the string section battling against the rest. It was difficult to make out who won, but when someone hits you it's the punch that counts, not which fist delivers it.

The Steve Gibbons Band reassured their promise in an accomplished opening set. The capabilities of both bands ensure an exciting evening's entertainment and a hot tour.

DAVID BROWN

Electric magic

by David Brown

TO BEAM or not to beam that is the question!

When you've gone to a lot of trouble, not to mention expense, featuring a laser light show in your act, it's a bit much when someone comes along and says it can't be done.

That was the problem facing Electric Light Orchestra at their recent London tour date. The band said let there be light, but the GLC said "No way".

"We were very disappointed about that," apologised drummer Bev Bevan. "I don't understand the technical side, but we had a qualified operator who was licenced to do it, from the States, so I'm sure there was no danger

"The lasers have been in use without trouble on our last tour in America and on most of the British dates. But what can you do?

Amazing

"We were particularly sorry about London because there was a TV crew getting in the way too. But the amazing thing was that the show still went well."

A chance to see ELO on tour is something of a rarity in itself now in this country, since the call of America is so strong.

"There's no way we could have made money touring here," said Bev. "It costs us money. There are seven of us in the band plus all the crew, equipment and so on. The funny thing is that a lot of people still think you make a fortune touring here.

"As far as we are concerned we like to play to please the fans. It's a loyalty thing. And when we do play we like to make an impression."

They certainly made an impression with the recent tour. It will be the New Year at least until we see them again. Until then there is a new album to be finished off in Munich, then back across the Atlantic to keep the customers satisfied over there.

Currently going up the US LP charts is an ELO compilation 'Ole ELO', which goes from '10538 Overture' onwards. Britain has often been slow to pick up on some of the band's material which has had great success in America, but renewed interest was heralded by their last album, from which we've had three popular singles — 'Night Rider', 'Evil Woman' and 'Strange Magic'.

The band still regard the UK as home though, with Bev and guitarist / vocalist Jeff Lynne still living close to their native Birmingham. But they were a little taken aback with the heatwave in Britain, since their last Transatlantic tour had been their "coldest ever" with some Candian gigs being 10 degrees under.

"We were literally dying with flu," says Bev. "At one place I got three roadies standing behind me in case I keeled over. Of course, on the next American tour it'll be red hot."

Shame

Anyone who has seen the band will know that Bev surrounds himself with masses of percussion instruments, including a giant drum kit, timpani and a huge gong. And unlike a lot of drummers who use them just for show, he actually plays them all.

"It would be a shame not to make use of them when you have them," he admits.

"And we get so much equipment given to us now it's unbelievable. It makes you think of the times when you had to scrape together two quid to pay off the installments on the gear. Then when you can afford it the companies give you it."

ELO: rare treat

Being part of a band that makes lavish use of orchestration, he has plenty of room to manoeuvre, though he doesn't go in for flashy solos, being a consistent worker rather than one who only has the occasional flash of inspiration.

"I think drum solos are really boring," he says. "I mean they are alright from a technical aspect but not to listen for any length of time.

"We used to have one in the Move days, but in ELO we've got a violin and cello solo, not many bands can boast that."

Bev was at one time thinking of pooling the talents of several top league drummers for a possible album of jazz drum classics.

"Roger Taylor of Queen was really keen," said Bev. "And I'd thought of Ian Paice, Aynsley Dunbar, John Bonham, but the problem was trying to fit it in with all our work.

"But Roger and I have pretty similar lifestyles and our tours coincide so we'll probably salvage something."

One drum record you are unlikely to hear is Bev's solo single 'Let There Be Drums', the Sandy Nelson oldie. "I recorded that about a year ago. It had always been my favourite and we thought it would be okay for the discos."

But when the original was reissued recently and died a death, it was decided that Bev's version was unlikely to do much better, so it was not released after all. It would have been his first solo- record and an instrumental one at that.

"I do a few bass harmonies," he says. "And in the Move days I sang a couple of numbers, sort of Johnny Cash Country and Western types.

"But now I'd rather leave the lead vocals to Jeff," he laughs.

Although Lynne was lead vocalist for most of the songs, Kelly Groucutt sang lead vocals on 'Poker' and (alternating with Lynne) on 'Nightrider'. This collaborative vocal approach injected the album with a dynamic and varied sound, extending upon the band's versatility.

The back cover of the record sleeve features an intriguing image of the band members pressing their faces against a glass panel. This visual suggests that they are observing the "electrocution" scene depicted on the front cover of the album. Notably, Richard Tandy is captured looking away in the photograph. According to Bev Bevan, Tandy didn't agree with the concept. Still though, it adds a distinctive touch to the album's overall visual presentation.

Released as a single in late 1975, 'Evil Woman' became ELO's first worldwide hit. Originally intending to use it as filler on *Face The Music*, Lynne wrote the song in under thirty minutes. With '10538 Overture (Live)' on the B-side, by early 1976, the song had placed within the top ten in several countries both sides of the Atlantic. It would be released again in 1978 on *The ELO EP*.

Billboard considered that 'Evil Woman' was "the perfect choice from the fast-rising new LP," adding that the song's title "works well as a hook." *Cash Box* said, "The electricity of this tune is grounded in twentieth century influence" and that "'Evil Woman' is sung with extreme commercial quality."

'Strange Music' was released as a single in February 1976. In the UK, the B-side was 'Showdown (Live)', and for the US, it was 'New World Rising'. It got to number thirty-eight in the UK, and to number fourteen in the US. *Record World* said, "An immaculate production by Jeff Lynne maintains the high calibre of the group's recorded work." *Billboard* called it an "easy rocker" with "smooth vocals and skilful string arrangements."

MELODY MAKER, December 4, 1976—Page 17
Soon, millions will hold A New World Record.
Electric Light Orchestra
A NEW WORLD RECORD
A NEW WORLD RECORD
Electric Light Orchestra
Album: UAG 30017 Cassette: TCK 30017
Including the hit single:
"LIVIN' THING"
UP 36184
Jet RECORDS
MARKETED & DISTRIBUTED BY UNITED ARTISTS RECORDS

Released as the third single from *Face The Music* — in spring 1976 in the UK, and then the following year in the US — 'Nightrider' (with a live version of 'Daybreaker' on the B-side) failed to chart. This was despite ELO's appearance on BBC's *Top Of The Pops* in April 1976, and, of course, their rising popularity overall.

The line-up that features on *Face The Music* would not only remain stable for the next five years, but would go on to be considered by many as ELO's classic line-up.

Released in autumn 1976 on Jet Records in the UK and by United Artists in the US, ELO's sixth studio album, *A New World Record*, features shorter, more pop-orientated songs than on their previous albums. Stylistically, the band would go on to continue in a similar vein for the rest of their career.

Lynne himself considered that around this time, he was at a new level in his songwriting abilities: "The songs started to flow and most of them came quickly to me. To have all those hits, it was just amazing really. Going from doing okay for probably three or four years to suddenly being in the big time, it was a strange but great thing."

ELO's second album to be recorded at Musicland Studios in Munich, *A New World Record* marked a pivotal shift for the band in terms of commercial success, particularly in the UK. Unlike their previous three studio albums, which had made little impact in their home country, in getting to number six, *A New World Record* achieved significant success by becoming ELO's first top ten album in the UK. It also achieved global acclaim and received multi-platinum certification in both the UK and the US (where it got to number five).

Within its first year of release, the album sold an impressive five-million units worldwide. Notably, its cover art introduced the ELO logo (designed by Kosh) for the first time — a design element that would become a consistent feature on most of the group's subsequent releases.

Dana Productions Inc.

Electric Light Orchestra was short-circuited by competition

It wasn't a night for electric charge

By BOB ROSS
St. Petersburg Times Staff Writer

ROSS ON MUSIC
opinion

Tuesday was a poor choice of evenings for a rock concert at the Bayfront Center Arena.

Suncoast rock fans tend to avoid spending $6 on a week night for a less than spectacular attraction. The Festival of States night parade and fireworks display just blocks away provided stiff competition for the attention of young music fans, particularly those who are members of participating high school bands.

And the recent announcement of an impending St. Petersburg visit by Bob Dylan knocked the rest of the ticket-sales market into a cocked hat, promoter Scott Stevens said Tuesday night as he watched about 3,500 patrons trickle into the arena.

THERE WERE PLENTY of excuses, but only one reason for the small turnout at the Electric Light Orchestra (ELO) concert. Not that many people care $6 worth about the group.

ELO is electric, it is light, and it could be called an orchestra, with two cellos and a violin complementing the standard heavy-metal guitar-bass-drums-keyboard quartet.

But a stringy gimmick does not a super-group make.

Led by Jeff Lynn, erstwhile mover of The Move (British standouts of the mod era largely ignored in the U.S.A.), ELO presented a predictable program of low-key rocking and high-gear fiddling around.

Boosted by commercial success with such smooth singles as "Evil Woman" and "Strange Magic," ELO seems to be concentrating on its new-found mellow image. Ballroom lighting and suavely clad musicians were welcomed enthusiastically by the small but dedicated cadre of Electric Light-ers.

A SEEMINGLY endless hour from Journey, a mind-numbing high-volume quartet of rock-and-roll castoffs (two from Santana, one from Steve Miller and a long-time drummer named Aynsley Dunbar who should know better), opened the show.

Despite intensive promotion from its record company, Journey is a group that has yet to find a musical groove. Tooth-shattering volume combined with droning repetition made this band's set rank with a boiler-factory tour in terms of pleasantness.

The whole Journey excursion seemed to be toward a vein of metallic rock that has been musically bankrupt for years.

BUT ELO, of course, sounded good by comparison.

Starting with material from their new, highly commercial album, ELO mixed pseudo-classical string chords with more or less traditional British rock riffs.

Unlike many bands with string sections and classy backgrounds, ELO is not pretentious. A loose, humorous attitude on stage makes ELO fun to watch even when their musical voltage lags.

Considering it was a mediocre evening for a show, the Electric Light Orchestra filled their amps with wattage, and received volts of confidence from the audience.

Electric Laser ban

ELO HAD an unexpected change of programme at the weekend when they appeared at the London New Victoria. The Greater London Council banned them from using the laser beam as part of the lights during their show, saying that the lights were dangerous.

ELO, who have used the lights throughout their British tour and on 68 dates in America, had to go without them.

EVENING MAIL, MONDAY, MAY 10, 1976

DAVID GRITTEN meets the man who switched on Electric Light Orchestra

Striking gold . . .

ONCE UPON a time on a Birmingham council estate, a smart kid called Jeff Lynne had a bright idea.

Why, he wondered, had no one ever merged pop and classical music by arranging pop tunes with lavish string backings, using cellos, violas and violins.

Years later, that was the bright idea which finally switched on the Electric Light Orchestra. And it took Jeff Lynne, the boy from Shard End, Birmingham, to a life of affluence and fame.

Now ELO sell millions of albums throughout the world, spend half their time in America, and enjoy massive critical acclaim.

Lynne is one of a highly talented generation of Brum pop artists, all now in the late 20's or early 30's, who have scaled the heights in the world of rock.

He is a very down to earth character, though, despite the riches, fame and travel.

We're talking in Quince's, a select club for gentlemen in London, W.1., just off Harley Street.

The occasion is a reception to award ELO two gold discs for a million sales of their last two albums "Eldorado" and "Face The Music."

It's very plush. Italian waiters hover attentively. The wine is good. The food is tasty and rich.

"It's given me an upset stomach," Jeff confesses.

Then there's a publicity stunt when six scantily dressed girls, sprayed all over in gold, present the group with gold records.

Jeff laughs and smiles for pictures, but he casts his eyes heavenwards in mock wonderment at it all.

ELO tend to take more seriously than these high life trappings important things like music and football.

Soccer

The music we all know about. But there is fierce competition inside the group between Blues fanatic Jeff, and Wolves supporter, drummer Bev Bevan.

It's more important to the group than you might imagine.

At last year's ELO Birmingham concert, the audience was littered with soccer stars like Trevor Francis, John Richards, Steve Kindon and Roger Hynd.

Bev is on the other side of the room, telling D.J. Bob Harris: "Sorry I couldn't make it Tuesday, but I HAD to go up to see Wolves and Liverpool. Tragedy they went down, wasn't it?" While Jeff is muttering: "I don't care about fair play. As long as the Blues stayed up."

And he admits: "One of the greatest thrills of my life was training with the Blues lads, playing head tennis with them.

"Funny isn't it. All the footballers I know want to make a record, and all the musicians want a League game!"

He now lives on a 10-acre farm near Stourport, Worcestershire.

"Best thing I ever did, buying that," he says. "It's lovely and peaceful, and I write all my songs there.

"My mum still lives in Shard End though. She'll be delighted by all this, because she always reads the Mail."

It was through the Mail that his career kicked off. He answered an advertisement for a "keen young lead guitarist" with Mike Sheridan's Night Riders, and got the job.

He had watched them when they played Shard End Community Centre. "I couldn't believe how good they were," he says.

Strings

Roy Wood had been in the Night Riders, too, and after Jeff had a spell as leader and writer for the imaginative but underrated Idle Race Group, he joined Roy and Bev in the Move.

But in commercial terms, the Move were on the skids, and it was from the need for a new group concept the ELO was born in 1972.

Their use of strings, and classically trained musicians, was revolutionary at the time.

"Roy was better known than me, and everyone assumed ELO was his idea," said Jeff.

"But I was writing most of their songs."

And within a few months, Roy left ELO to leave Jeff their undisputed front man.

Support

They've never looked back. They have gained an enormous following in America, where their albums and singles automatically make the Top 10.

In fact, they're far more popular there than here, which bewilders them.

"We played Philadelphia a while back and walked on stage to find an audience of 20,000," says Jeff. "I thought, blimey, the Beatles must be topping the bill, but it was us they wanted.

"In America, the audiences are better, and they don't categorise music, they just accept it if they like it.

"Over here, we fall between stools, and fans don't seem to know how to regard us.

"I think ELO music is distinctive. It has a lot of discipline, it's tightly arranged, not aimless. We couldn't just go on stage and improvise for 20 minutes."

They are basically a conventional four-man group with three extra musicians on electrified cellos and violin.

Admittedly, the idea of the seven man "orchestra" might be hard to adjust to for first-time audiences.

There is no stranger sight in pop than seeing classically trained Hugh McDowell whirling his royal blue cello round after a solo.

The tops

But they are aiming to crack the British market.

After their American tour of 63 working days out of the last 75, they cancelled their British tour until next month because they felt they would be "jaded."

"We'll be in Birmingham next month," says Jeff. "We're always a bit nervous, but I love going back. I spend a lot of time abroad, but I think the Midlands is the greatest place there is."

JEFF LYNNE . . . front man of the Electric Light Orchestra. His pop career started when he answered a Mail advertisement for a lead guitarist.

Meet the rest of the magnificent seven

● Bev Bevan . . . drums.

● Hugh McDowall . . . cello.

● Kelly Groucutt . . . bass and vocals.

● Mik Kaminsky . . . violin.

● Richard Tandy . . . keyboards.

● Melvyn Gale . . . cello.

* * *

By WARREN GERDS
Press-Gazette Staff Writer

Electric Light Orchestra — A NEW WORLD RECORD (United Artists UA-LA 679-G)

Jeff Lynne is the brains of Electric Light Orchestra. He's got quite an imagination.

On "A New World Record," he collects all the major credits — for music, lyrics and production.

What Lynne is is a chameleon. He changes his colors at will to suit the musical styles he's into — basically classical, rock and pop.

Often those changes come in the course of one song. It's when Electric Light Orchestra is multiple-shifting that it's at its best.

Pieces like "Tightrope" open with a big, symphonic sound. Then they reverse directions to rock, then go back and forth from there on. It makes for fun and fascinating listening.

To a degree, Electric Light Orchestra owes deference to a lot of earlier creators. Like the Beatles and Chuck Berry. Some of the vocals are Lennonesque, and "Rockaria" is a direct descendant of "Roll Over Beethoven."

While Lynne is clever with his rock-symphonic creations, he also knows which side his bread is buttered on. He has an ear for the sellable, commercial sound.

Example: "Livin' Thing," which is getting AM airplay. In it, Lynne opts for a simpler, more straightfoward style. While it is not the best cut on the album (with its sharpness in the chorus), it has strong mass appeal.

Another AM contender is "Do Ya," where whirling rock guitars, Moody Blues-like unison vocals and Mick Jaggerish solo singing dominate.

Overall, "A New World Record" is top shelf stuff.

* * *

ELO sticks to winning formula

By Bill Provick

Entertainment
pages 82-85

Imagine hauling a massive rig over God knows how many miles through an incredibly vicious storm — mere rumours of which had kept Ottawans wincing and bracing themselves all day — knowing thousands of people are depending on you.

And when you finally do arrive — unavoidably late – you find that not only has your main workday just begun but the key part of it has been condensed to a mere fraction of the time normally allowed for completion.

Roadies – the hard-working, crazy-living work crews repsonsible for transporting, unpacking, erecting, dismantling and repacking the tons of equipment a rock band uses — usually arrive in town the day of a show and spend several hours setting up in the afternoon. The band and the technicians run through a sound check and the equipment is then pushed to the back of the stage, hopefully all set to go when showtime rolls around.

Showtime for Electric Light Orchestra's (ELO) return engagement at the Civic Centre Tuesday night was set back an hour due to the storm that immobilized most of southern Ontario. Even then – judging from the huge transport trailer frantically trying to dodge its way into the parking lot as I arrived – ELO's roadies barely made it in time.

The boisterous crowd of 7,000 — who even applauded thunderously the pre-show announcement of upcoming concerts (Genesis, April 3; Supertramp, April 21; Kiss, April 22) – didn't seem to mind and gave substitute warm-up act Rush a surprisingly strong reception.

Rush turned in a creditable but not especially exciting 45-minute set, coming across strangely muted for a supposedly high-energy rock trio.

Though the attention of much of the audience wandered quite noticeably, the band drew a fairly satisfactory response and even drew an encore when the lighting crew was slow in raising the house lights.

Everyone seemed quite prepared for a long intermission, realizing the ELO roadies had tons of equipment to erect once Rush's crew had cleared the deck. But before anyone had a chance to get restless – in slightly less than an hour — the roadies had not only arranged all the equipment on stage (more than usual as ELO is a seven-man band) but even found time to install two searchlights (as opposed to spotlights), a massive backdrop and a huge hanging crystal globe.

This extra equipment was used to glorious effect when ELO took the stage and opened with the majestic *Eldorado Overture.*

From there it was a steady, 90-minute stream of old and new compositions that consistently delighted the crowd.

A rock band runs a considerable risk taking to the stage cold — literally and figuratively – without a warm up and without a sound check. ELO occasionally got hung up with vocal difficulties, especially early in the show, but overall this concert was as good as — if not better than – the band's last appearance here.

What helped was the audience's recently acquired familiarity with newer material from the *Face The Music* album, including *Poker, Nightrider, Strange Magic* and perhaps the best tune of the evening, *Evil Woman.* Earlier works — especially *Eldorado, Can't Get It Out Of My Head* and *Showdown* were also well received.

In all ways, ELO stuck to its winning formula and simply performed its distinctive style of music to the best of its abilities. As usual this remarkable mixture of the surging mellowness of strings (electric violin and cellos) with the electric excitment of more standard instruments (guitar, bass, drums and assorted keyboards) topped off by captivating vocals proved easy to take yet a keen pleasure to experience.

ELO capped a rousing finish with an even more rousing encore — its trademark, a frantic, personalized rendition of *Roll Over Beethoven.*

I'm sure if Beethoven had heard it, he certainly would have rolled over. But I'm also sure that had he lived in our time, he too would have liked it — ELO are that good.

Later going on to agree with a journalist's comment that *A New World Record* was a commercial turning point for ELO, Lynne said; "Just prior to that, we'd had two really big hits with 'Evil Woman' and 'Strange Magic', both from *Face The Music*. We'd got a different line-up together and started doing these American tours, which turned out amazingly well. We seemed like such a strange group for an American audience, with two cellos, a violin, Mellotron and a bit of French horn. It was just an odd sound."

A New World Record spawned four hit singles. 'Livin' Thing' was a transatlantic top ten hit. 'Telephone Line' earned the distinction of being the band's first gold US single. There was also 'Rockaria!' and 'Do Ya' — a rendition of the 1972 single by The Move.

The first single released from the album, 'Livin' Thing' had 'Fire On High' as the B-side in the UK, and in the US, 'Ma-Ma-Ma Belle'. The *Los Angeles Times* called it an "extremely catchy record that has all the vocal and instrumental hooks to keep you listening." *Cash Box* said that "a diabolical arrangement hits hard along with some ever-ready harmonies which sew this record up into sure hit potential." *Record World* called it a "Jeff Lynne masterwork."

With 'Nightrider' on the B-side, 'Do Ya' got to number twenty-four in the US when released in early 1977. *Billboard* praised its "catchy melody line." The final single released by The Move, prior to recording the song for *A New World Record*, ELO had been playing it as part of their live performances from 1973. Also, they had incorporated the riff from 'Do Ya' into live renditions of '10538 Overture', a version of which can be found on their 1974 live album, *The Night The Light Went On In Long Beach.*

The Electric Light Orchestra . . . two nights of classics, rock and laser lights at The Spectrum

Electric Light Flips Switch, Dazzling Fans at Spectrum

ELECTRIC LIGHT ORCHESTRA and STEVE HILLAGE. At the Spectrum.

By MATT DAMSKER
Of the Bulletin Staff

ONE OF BRITAIN'S most persistent rock groups, the Electric Light Orchestra (ELO) appears to have reached a peak of popularity in this country. Impressively, the septet drew a total of about 38,000 fans to two Spectrum concerts this past weekend — feisty, enjoyable performances marked by spirited showmanship, a succession of crowd-pleasing hit songs and an often dazzling incorporation of laser-beam lighting effects.

Indeed, one has to admire the way in which ELO, under the aegis of songwriter-singer-guitarist Jeff Lynne, has wrung so much success from its formula. Lynne's infectious pop-rock tunes may be highly derivative — some seem almost note-for-note recreations of Beattle classics — but their sound is most distinctive. It results from a blend of multi-layered vocal and electronic textures, bottom-heavy rock 'n roll, and the baroque, symphonic timbres of cellos and violin.

"Symphonic as it may be, ELO never allows its "classical" dimension to get in the way of its pop-rock appeal, although the group's debt to the classics is gleefully acknowledged by such set pieces as violinist Mik Kaminski's fleet rendering of "Hungarian Rhapsody" — while a laser beams shifting pinpoints of color upon his violin. As for that, one suspects that lasers are proving more of a crutch than a breakthrough for such threatrically limited groups as ELO, but even so their concentrated intensities can lend hypnotic focus to an otherwise plain presentation, and ELO is at once tasteful and imaginative in exploiting the trend.

At the same time ELO rouses the audience with tightly controlled but far from sterile versions of its most successful material. From the swirling, extended fantasy of "Can't Get It Out Of My Head" to the bubble-gummy rock of "Livin' Thing," "Evil Woman" or "Do Ya," the group strikes a common denominator of rhythm and melody that can't be denied. Whatever ELO may not be, its music certainly works.

With 'Poker' on the B-side, 'Rockaria!' got to number nine in the UK and also fared well in Europe and Australia when it was released as a single in early 1977. The song features the soprano vocals of Mary Thomas. "I'm really pleased with 'Rockaria!'," Lynne told *Melody Maker.* "It's a tongue-in-cheek look at classical rock, but it is a rocker and I think it's the best in the rock tradition that we've done. It's a new-style rocker."

A song about a guy anticipating a call from a girl, in May 1977, 'Telephone Line' was the final single to be released from *A New World Record*. It got to number eight in the UK and to number seven in the US. In the US, 'Poor Boy (The Greenwood)' featured on the B-side, whilst in the UK, 'King Of The Universe' was included as well as the latter. At the time of recording the song, anticipating the album to resonate more with listeners in the US, Lynne sought to replicate the sound of an American ring tone rather than a British one. He recalled; "To get the sound on the beginning — the American telephone sound — we phoned from England to America to a number that we knew nobody would be at, to just listen to it for a while. On the Moog, we recreated the sound exactly by tuning the oscillators to the same notes as the ringing of the phone."

A New World Record was given a positive welcome from the music press, both in the UK and in the US. NME referred to it as "a very ambitious album," adding that "Lynne and his band are in the front rank of the nation's rock experts, and it's time their standing was properly acknowledged at home."

Sounds opined; "Lynne has captured the essential atmosphere of sophisticated pop without sounding overblown or cheap. Each of the nine tracks is immediate, commercial, professional."

Record Mirror said, "Combining electric guitars with highbrow symphonies is a pretty crazy combination, but for the ELO it works. Often the music borders on clumsiness and the lyrics are sometimes silly, but the band's sense of fun carries them through."

June 25, 1977
15p
Record Mirror
CLASH
in colour
ELO
on the end of the line
OK CLEVER CLOGS
Here's your chance to win £50
Turn to page 10
GENESIS
HOT RODS
PISTOLS v PEOPLE
You have your say
Pic: San Emerson

Melody Maker considered that Lynne and Roy Wood had originally formed ELO with the intent of being "a group that would merge the excitement and colour of rock and roll with the clear lines of classical music," and that *A New World Record* was "the closest that the Electric Light Orchestra have come to realising this." The publication went on to say that the album "takes a giant leap forward... the most striking progression on this album is the use of orchestra and choir. Strings are no longer a novelty... *A New World Record* is ELO's best album in its seven-year history, the most complete of them all. They're a band who haven't yet gained the attention in this country that they deserve. Acquiring this album would be a fine way to change all that."

Rolling Stone enthused; "By Christmas, *A New World Record* should be a staple in a million homes." The reviewer also noted; "Lynne has always been rather deft with the melodic hook, and both 'Livin' Thing' and 'So Fine' are irresistible additions to his list of catchiest tunes. Numbers like 'Mission (A World Record)' and 'Shangri-La' continue the history of classy orchestral stylings that really rock."

To support the release of *A New World Record*, ELO embarked on a tour of the US. It spanned from September 1976 to April 1977, with a brief break in December. During this time, the band also made an appearance at the American Music Awards show on 31st January 1977. Additionally, they performed a single show in San Diego in August 1977, marking a special one-off event during this period.

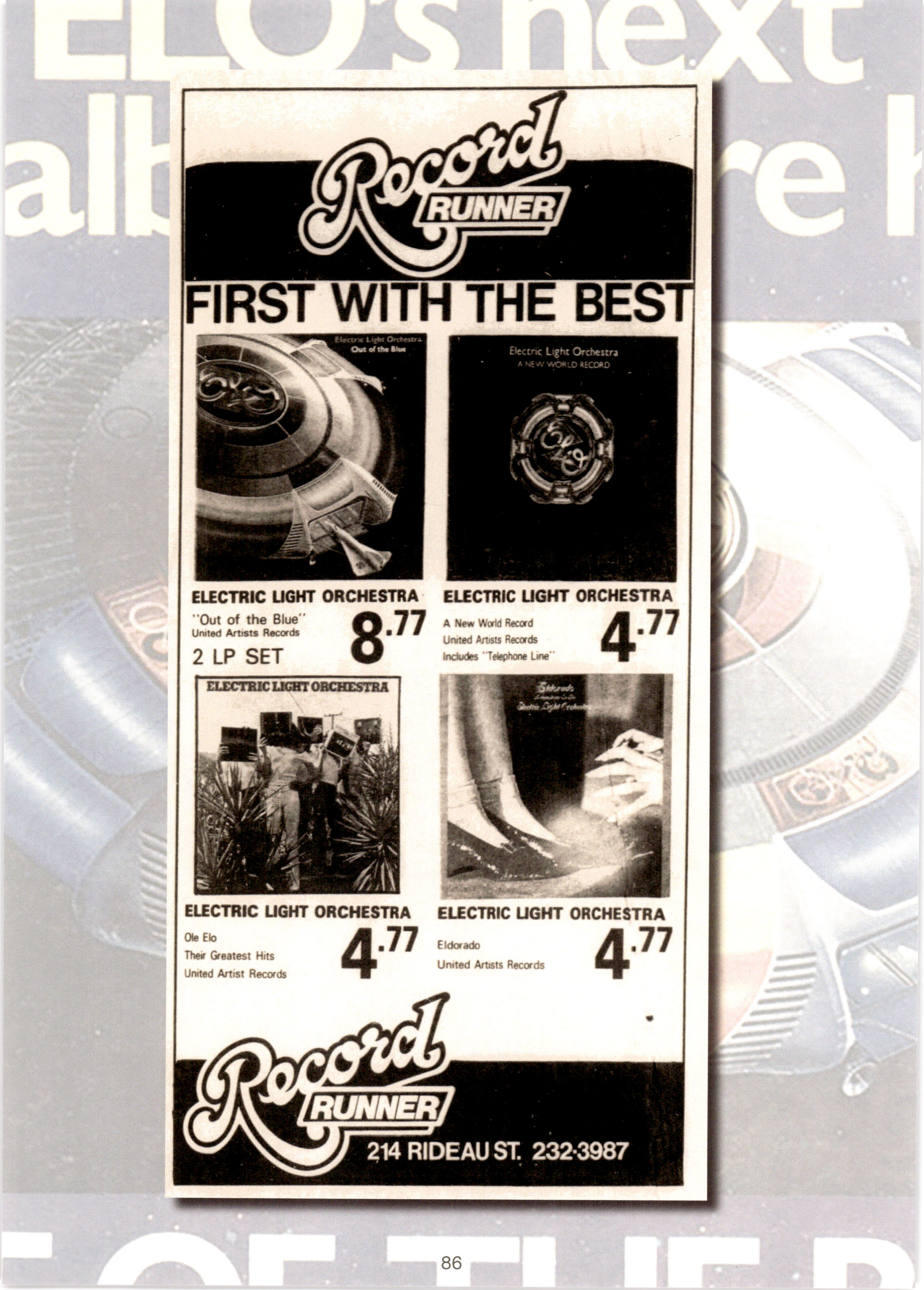
ELO's next
Record RUNNER
FIRST WITH THE BEST
Electric Light Orchestra
Out of the Blue
Electric Light Orchestra
A NEW WORLD RECORD
ELECTRIC LIGHT ORCHESTRA
"Out of the Blue"
United Artists Records
2 LP SET
8.77
ELECTRIC LIGHT ORCHESTRA
A New World Record
United Artists Records
Includes "Telephone Line"
4.77
ELECTRIC LIGHT ORCHESTRA
ELECTRIC LIGHT ORCHESTRA
Ole Elo
Their Greatest Hits
United Artist Records
4.77
ELECTRIC LIGHT ORCHESTRA
Eldorado
United Artists Records
4.77
Record RUNNER
214 RIDEAU ST. 232-3987

Based on an interview with *Sounds* in late 1976, it's clear that each musician had a vital role to play. "We get plenty of opportunities on stage," said Mik Kaminski, "because both of us do a solo of our own — virtually going on for as long as we like, and playing what we like. You use your own judgement as to whether or not the audience is getting bored, and if they do get bored, it's your problem, so it's a good outlet." Hugh McDowell said, "The solos go down really well with the audiences, considering that we're doing some pretty freaky stuff. When you can get thirty-thousand people waiting on the end of one note, it's amazing."

"It's difficult to say why ELO never broke through in their own country before this year," *Melody Maker* opined in April 1977. "The quality of the music has been unusually high for the past three years, and the response was relatively low for two of them. The band have never totally neglected the cult following here, but the pedestrian fashion in which Britain has accepted the ELO will no doubt lead to some reaction when it comes to plotting out tours." Lynne responded to this with, "I'm just chuffed. It's suddenly happened, and I accept that. I don't look any deeper than that."

ELO's seventh studio release, double album *Out Of The Blue*, had its beginnings in a charming Swiss chalet perched above the village of Bassins in the midst of the Jura Mountains. Whilst there, Lynne was determined to write a sufficient amount of new material to craft a double album. The success of *A New World Record* had catapulted ELO to global superstardom, leading to heightened expectations from their record company, critics, and the band's millions of fans.

"I rented this little chalet in Switzerland, on the mountains just beyond Lake Geneva," said Lynne. "I rented this gear from a little shop in a village, a little music shop, with a Revox tape recorder, an electric piano — I had my guitar there — and just sat there to try and write. For two weeks, I came up with nothing — and I only had four weeks to write this double album! I was sort of thinking, 'Bloody 'ell, maybe I can't come up with anything'."

ELECTRIC LIGHT ORCHESTRA'S
NEW DOUBLE ALBUM

OUT OF THE BLUE'
LBUM UAR100 · CASSETTE 2TCK100 · CARTRIDGE 28XU100
Jet RECORDS
Marketed by UA Records Ltd.

ELO's next
two albums are here.
OUT OF THE BLUE
A new album by Electric Light Orchestra is always a special event.
Now, out of the blue, comes even more ELO than you bargained for.
Two records, seventeen new songs by the most
important group recording today.
All songs written and produced by JEFF LYNNE.
On Jet Records and Tapes Distributed by United Artists Records.
Jet Records
©1977 United Artists Music and Records Group, Inc.

October 15, 1977 SOUNDS Page 31
ELECTRIC LIGHT ORCHESTRA'S
NEW SINGLE
TURN TO STONE
(FIRST 100,000 COPIES IN FULL COLOUR BAG)
UP 36313
FROM THEIR FORTHCOMING ALBUM 'OUT OF THE BLUE'

Following meticulous preparations that included crafting orchestral and choral arrangements in collaboration with Richard Tandy and conductor Louis Clark (as well as rehearsals with other band members) in May 1977, ELO went to Munich's Musicland Studios to record *Out Of The Blue*, where they worked with their trusted sound engineer, Reinhold Mack.

"I just got to like the studio," said Lynne. "I liked where it was because there was a good football pitch out the back for having a break. There's one great thing about when you make records, it's lovely to work for like four or five hours and then go out and have a good game of football because it really clears your mind. Then carry on working into the early hours."

Accompanied by an extensive and highly publicised marketing campaign that boldly declared "ELO's next two albums are here", *Out Of The Blue* was released in October 1977. It was a resounding success, flying off the shelves of stores and swiftly becoming the highest-selling ELO album. A year later, a staggering ten-million copies of *Out Of The Blue* had been sold worldwide, solidifying its status as a monumental achievement in the band's history.

Whilst considering that "to better *A New World Record* is a great achievement," *Record Mirror* called *Out Of The Blue* "almost a masterpiece and easily one of the best albums this year."

As well as *Out Of The Blue* itself getting to number four in the UK and US, and firmly into the top ten in Australia, Canada and numerous countries in Europe, the album was host to several high-performing singles.

'Turn To Stone' was released as a single the same month the album came out. With 'Mister Kingdom' on the B-side, it got to number eighteen in the UK, and to number thirteen in the US. *Billboard* called it a "driving, high energy rocker," whilst *Record World* considered that it "clearly bears the Jeff Lynne stamp."

With ‘One Summer Dream’ on the B-side, released in January 1978, ‘Mr. Blue Sky’ got to number six in the UK and to number thirty-five in the US (where it was met with critical acclaim). *Cash Box* said ‘Mr. Blue Sky’ “features a characteristically full sound and effective use of breaks” and that “fast pace, airy singing and strings provide musical dramatics.” *Billboard* described the song’s beat as “catchy” and said that as a whole, the piece builds from a “thumping intro” to a “harmonic operatic” ending. *Record World* opined; “This up-tempo tune guarantees Lynne’s legend as both writer and producer and shows off ELO’s unique sound.”

Of writing ‘Mr. Blue Sky’, and on how his writing for the rest of *Out Of The Blue* progressed thereafter, Lynne recalled; “The weather had been really bad and then one day I got up and it was fantastic, the sun was brilliant and shining, all the mountains were lit up and this mist had gone away. It was gorgeous and I came up with ‘Mr. Blue Sky’. I just kept coming up with songs then. They just came really quickly and I came up with about fourteen in the two weeks after the first empty two weeks.”

In May 1978 with ‘Eldorado’ on the B-side, ‘Wild West Hero’ was released as a single in the UK where it got to number six.

Released as a single in September 1978, ‘Sweet Talkin’ Woman’ had ‘Bluebird Is Dead’ as the B-side in the UK, and ‘Fire On High’ in the US. Getting to number six in the UK and to number seventeen in the US, the single was met with positive critical response. *Billboard* called it a “catchy rocker characterised by semi-classical elements.” *Cash Box* praised its “syncopated harmonies and full-bodied instrumental accompaniments.”

With ‘The Whale’ on the B-side, ‘It’s Over’ was released as a single in October 1978. *Record World* welcomed it as “a classic ELO single keyed by Jeff Lynne’s unique vocals and production techniques.”

Bev Bevan during the
New World Record Tour, 1977.
(Pictorial Press Ltd / Alamy Stock Photo)

PAGE 62 CALENDAR Los Angeles Times SUNDAY, JANUARY 23, 1977

Pop Music

Jeff Lynne Orchestrates ELO's Success

BY RICHARD CROMELIN

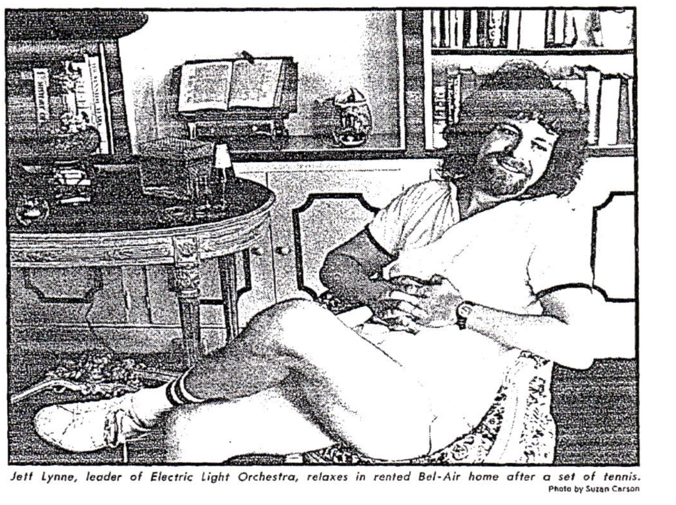

Jeff Lynne, leader of Electric Light Orchestra, relaxes in rented Bel-Air home after a set of tennis.
Photo by Suzan Carson

● Most attempts to combine rock and orchestral formats have led to uncomfortable mergers at best, and more often to utterly pretentious and insignificant music. The exceptions—Procol Harum's live album, the Beatles' middle period and early Moody Blues—share an affinity for the tight, solid song. Most senior rock fans can hum "Knights in White Satin" or "Strawberry Fields." But they would be hard pressed to recall a few bars of "Deep Purple With the London Symphony" or a 10-minute Keith Emerson solo.

Although classical-oriented performers like Rick Wakeman and Emerson, Lake & Palmer command large audiences within the progressive-to-heavy-metal wing, their realm is quite distinct from the pop mainstream. But with the smashing success of the Electric Light Orchestra's "A New World Record," the rock band-orchestra marriage has made its first assertive move into the Elton John world of hit singles and widespread radio play. One crucial reason for its across-the-board popularity: ELO concentrates on the song as a song, not as a secondary appendage to an orchestral concept.

"Before 'El Dorado' the direction was very mixed" explains ELO's leader, Jeff Lynne, relaxing in a rented Bel-Air home after a set of tennis. "On 'ELO II' and stuff like that I didn't know which way to go. I was trying to write stuff that wasn't me. It was a lot of waffle, as opposed to good tunes. A lot of it was based on instrumental, avant-garde stuff that I didn't particularly like, but thought I should like. The songs I'm writing now are 10 times better than what I was writing then."

The 29-year-old Lynne doesn't read or write music, so it's understandable that he would regard the pop tune and the melodic hook as the basic taking-off points. That penchant for the commercial rock song can be traced to Lynne's musical upbringing in Birmingham, the Detroit of England, where the favorites were tuneful harmony groups like the Beach Boys, the Four Seasons and the city's own Hollies.

The initial impetus for the Electric Light Orchestra was the Beatles' adventurous "I Am the Walrus" period. Lynne joined Birmingham's legendary Move in order to team with that rock band's Roy Wood and Bev Bevan (ELO's drummer) on a project that would follow that path and, further, transfer it to the stage without loss of quality. Wood left after the first ELO album. The band stumbled until it found the proper technology for the live sound and Lynne finally came up with that elusive direction.

Lynne singles out "El Dorado," the group's fourth album as the turning point. "That was the first time I'd used the orchestra and choir," he says. "It gave me a lot more confidence. It was a giant step, really, and from then on I've seen what direction to go in.

"The album before that, 'On the Third Day,' was the first time I tried a concept side, so that was really the first step. I finished it and I suddenly realized that I'd got the idea for this big orchestra next time. I said' 'That's it!' Because I was fed up with double-tracking these cellos and violins 20 times to make it sound like an orchestra. It's a step every time, because you learn more about what orchestras and choirs can actually do. It's all becoming a lot easier to work with."

As Lynne gains assurance in his blend of rock and classical elements, the Electric Light Orchestra steadily transcends the "classical-rock" lable. "I don't think that's us anymore," Lynne remarks. "It's too restrictive. I don't think we're in a category that narrow."

Indeed, ELO has moved well beyond its initial progressive/Anglophile cult following and is now scoring primarily through its infectious pop-rock aspects—melody, vocals, production—and by its deft integration of the strings into its rough rock sound. "A lot of people who use big orchestras tend to use them as a separate entity," Lynne points out. "But on the majority of our songs I can hear all the parts when I write it."

Lynne is an affable fellow, but he isn't given to expansive dissertation on his music or to speculation on future developments. He does, however, indicate a keen interest in incorporating more electronic technology, and he's already begun formulating the next step for ELO. "I don't think 'A New World Record' is necessarily the start of a trend to shorter songs," he says. "That was one album. The next one will probably be a concept again."

That album, to be recorded in Germany after the current tour, will tie in with a feature film in which, according to manager Don Arden, "the band will be presented in a specially animated form."

THE POPLIGHT

"A New World Record," Electric Light Orchestra. United Artists UA LA 679. The English band leans on a lot of obvious influences (from the Beatles to the Bee Gees), but the result is such a bright, appealing collection that it's hard to scold the group.

"Hotel California," the Eagles. Asylum 7E 1084. Rather than soothe or gently stir as in the past, the Eagles' objective this time is to jar. It's a bold, adventurous work that deals with greed, ambition and desire in the promised land of California.

"Night Moves," Bob Seger. Capitol ST 11557. In one of the year's most enjoyable collections, Seger shows humor, point of view and an occasional evocativeness that give his work far more dimension than most high-energy rockers.

"Rock and Roll Over," Kiss. Casablanca NBLP 7037. Because of the plunder and lightning of its stage show, there might be the tendency to dismiss the group's albums as some incidental by-products. But the demon clowns' sixth LP offers some irresistible junk-food boogie.

"Wings Over America," Paul McCartney & Wings. Capitol SWCO 11593. For the first time, a major rock star has put an entire concert into an album. The three record-set stand as an inviting souvenir of one of the most acclaimed tours of the '70s.

If "El Dorado," a lush, Beatles-influenced rock symphony, was a creative turning point for Lynne, it also served as a commercial breakthrough for the band as a whole. The album went Top 10 and, significantly, the score yielded a hit single in "Can't Get It Out of My Head." ELO's "El Dorado" tour in the fall of '74 —its fourth in a year but the first to be properly timed with an album release—formed a double punch and established a momentum that hasn't waned.

ELO, always a tireless touring band, began with the goal of covering as much American ground as possible and it remains a fixture on U.S. stages. Locally, the group is following hard on last summer's Universal Amphitheater stint with concerts at the Inglewood Forum on Thursday and Jan. 31.

"I should think we'll carry on for another 18 months," Don Arden says. "Eventually we've got to cool it off and do about 15 giant shows a year. I can't stand these people who do all this mystique bit—'Hey, man, we're gonna do an album in two years,' and all that. They get the fans at it and then they tease them. I can't really see the point in building up a giant following and then ignoring them."

Despite ELO's increasingly pervasive presence on the radio, its mounting sales and its high profile as a performing unit, it remains a rather faceless band, a group without a star. That reflects the nature of its leader, who is involved in the music to the exclusion of acting the part of the rock personality.

"Whenever I finish one album, I can't wait to start the next one," said Lynne, whose idea of heaven must be an eternal booking in the perfect studio. Lynne's duties in the Electric Light Orchestra include composition of words and music, collaboration on string arrangements, album production, lead vocals and guitar. Comanager Dave Arden theorizes that "everyone in the group is an extension of Jeff."

ELO keyboardist Richard Tandy is an integral part of the arrangement process, and all members (besides Lynne, Bevan and Tandy, the group consists of Mik Kaminski on violin, Hugh McDowell and Melvyn Gale on cellos and Kelly Groucutt on bass) contribute ideas during rehearsal, but there's no mistaking Lynne's dominant role.

"We all love playing together, and they're free to make albums on their own and do whatever they want," Lynne said in defense of his position of authority. "This is what I've always worked for. It's my group really, mine and Bev's. This is what we worked for, that's how it is and everybody accepts it." ●

Cromelin regularly reviews pop records and concerts for The Times.

Electric Light Flips Switch, Dazzling Fans at Spectrum

ELECTRIC LIGHT ORCHESTRA and STEVE HILLAGE. At the Spectrum.

By MATT DAMSKER
Of the Bulletin Staff

ONE OF BRITAIN'S most persistent rock groups, the Electric Light Orchestra (ELO) appears to have reached a peak of popularity in this country. Impressively, the septet drew a total of about 38,000 fans to two Spectrum concerts this past weekend — feisty, enjoyable performances marked by spirited showmanship, a succession of crowd-pleasing hit songs and an often dazzling incorporation of laser-beam lighting effects.

Indeed, one has to admire the way in which ELO, under the aegis of songwriter-singer-guitarist Jeff Lynne, has wrung so much success from its formula. Lynne's infectious pop-rock tunes may be highly derivative — some seem almost note-for-note recreations of Beattle classics — but their sound is most distinctive. It results from a blend of multi-layered vocal and electronic textures, bottom-heavy rock 'n roll, and the baroque, symphonic timbres of cellos and violin.

"Symphonic as it may be, ELO never allows its "classical" dimension to get in the way of its pop-rock appeal, although the group's debt to the classics is gleefully acknowledged by such set pieces as violinist Mik Kaminski's fleet rendering of "Hungarian Rhapsody" — while a laser beams shifting pinpoints of color upon his violin. As for that, one suspects that lasers are proving more of a crutch than a breakthrough for such threatrically limited groups as ELO, but even so their concentrated intensities can lend hypnotic focus to an otherwise plain presentation, and ELO is at once tasteful and imaginative in exploiting the trend.

At the same time ELO rouses the audience with tightly controlled but far from sterile versions of its most successful material. From the swirling, extended fantasy of "Can't Get It Out Of My Head" to the bubble-gummy rock of "Livin' Thing," "Evil Woman" or "Do Ya," the group strikes a common denominator of rhythm and melody that can't be denied. Whatever ELO may not be, its music certainly works.

'Light' in the distance

• Bev Bevan and Jeff Lynne

MIDLANDS superstars Jeff Lynne and Bev Bevan have been forced to become tax exiles — because they and the Electric Light Orchestra are so successful.

They are now spending only 60 days in Britain each year.

But as yet, neither of them has sold their Midlands homes — Jeff lives on a farm in Worcestershire, Bev in a large house in Moseley, Birmingham.

A third ELO member, Hugh McDowell, also now lives out of the country — on the West Coast of America in California.

★

Tony Brainsby, ELO's publicist, told me: "This is the first year Jeff and Bev have been forced to spend most of their time abroad — because last year was the first that ELO really started to sell in a big way in America."

As yet, I understand, neither Jeff nor Bev has established a permanent base abroad.

However, ELO has become a multi million dollar industry in the States. All their albums and singles are now assured of chart status and gold records.

Their tax difficulties will not hurt as much as they might, because they spend three or four months each year touring America in any case.

The band are now spending two months recording their next album in Munich, West Germany — the city where they also recorded their current hit LP, "A New World Record."

★

ELO's elevation to superstar status was gradual at first, but has accelerated in the last 18 months.

During that time, they have aimed — and succeeded — at establishing their American popularity. The huge sales of their last two albums "A New World Record" and "Face the Music" have confirmed this.

And in the meantime, they have enjoyed consistently popular sales of albums and singles in the less lucrative, but still important British market.

★

So for the time being, Jeff and Bev are spending most of the year living out of suitcases at various hotels.

While they undoubtedly earn a lot of money, it's an unhappy situation that most of our home grown pop stars are forced to stay away from Britain for most of the year.

For one thing, it limits the chances of British audiences — who helped them become superstars — to see them in live concerts.

Jeff cuts a solo single

JEFF Lynne, leader of the Electric Light Orchestra, temporarily leaves his group — for his first solo single.

It's called "Doin' That Crazy Thing," it's released next week on Jet Records — and it sounds like a surefire hit.

But whatever happens, the release of the single does not mean Jeff and E.L.O. are going their separate ways.

A spokesman for the group says: "The single is very much a one-off affair."

Be that as it may, Jeff persuaded **Elton John** to sit in on the session and play piano.

And if I'm not mistaken, Elton joins in on the vocals, too.

A catchy, danceable tune with an irresistable chorus.

"Doin' That Crazy Thing" could just do for summer 1977 what Elton and Kiki Dee's "Don't Go Breaking My Heart" did for summer 1976.

ELECTRIC LIGHT ORCHESTRA: "The Light Shines On" (Harvest).

JUST in case you thought the ELO was an overnight sensation, "The Ligh Shines On" is a collection of early material, circa 1971, and features the original line up of Roy Wood, Jeff Lynne and Bev. Bevan.

It's easy to see why they took so long to reach the top. The world just wasn't ready for them seven years ago.

What puzzles me is how a band can lose a musician of the calibre of Roy Wood and actually get better.

Jeff Lynne . . . Doin' That Crazy Thing . . . (UP 36281).

A POWERFUL little number from Jeff with some strong instrumental backing. A lot will depend on whether he can capture the exposure on the radio that a new record needs to launch it on the way to success.

Still I enjoyed it and thought that the overall back-up sound way very tight with a nice basic beat throughout.

By SCOTT CAIN

The major entertainment event of the week is a concert by the Electric Light Orchestra, the British rock 'n' roll group. The show is scheduled Thursday at 8 p.m. in the Omni.

Leo Sayer, who was previously announced as a costar, will not participate. Elliott Murphy has been added to the program in Sayer's place.

The Electric Light Orchestra is traveling with a major laser-light presentation, a spokesman states.

The band, which fuses classical elements with rock, is touring in connection with the album, "A New World Record," which continues a recent streak of ELO hits. A single called "Livin' Thing" has also been on the charts lately.

Electric Light at full power

ELECTRIC LIGHT ORCHESTRA

TURNTABLE by ROBIN ANDERSON

STUDENT prince of string-driven rock Jeff Lynne, the leading luminary with Electric Light Orchestra, gleaned a hatful of hit singles from "A New World Record."

"Out of the Blue" (Jet) may not yield the same harvest of immediate best-sellers but it's chock-full of astral surprises, burning through enough highlights to launch it into the vanguard of ELO's finest work ever.

Jeff Lynne's writing has rarely been bettered and his synthesis of rock's musical vocabulary with a host of classical and traditional catch-phrases — borrowed or stolen — accrues convincing originality under his spacious fresh-faced production.

The orchestral layering has bags of punchy internal combustion be it the gypsy-fired Tijuana soul and Buddy Holly pizzicato laced into "Across the Border" of the baroque rip-off licks that open "Sweet Talkin' Woman" or the rich tonescapes almost everywhere else.

Juxtaposed with Jeff's haze-edged harmonies, Richard Tandy's multi-strata keyboards and Bev Bevan's sizzling drum array, the effect is incurably addictive.

"Turn To Stone" starts the extravaganza in dead-eyed ELO fashion and is destined to be a classic. A menacing hook spikes "Night In The City" with awesome vibrancy while "Jungle" sweats gloriously amid torrid equatorial swamps as Tarzan swings through the trees.

Dreamy

Ballads like echo-plex "Starlight" and autumn-hued "It's Over" plus the dreamy grandeur of "Believe Me Now" and a slow-motion Beatles-trip "Big Wheels" reflect the band in mellower mood and happily meant the difference between two sides and four.

Side three, subtitled "Concerto for a Rainy Day" ranges from big keyboard cascades for "Standin' In the Rain" to a hyper-melodic static storm generated by "Summer and Lightning" and a churning roller "Mr. Blue Sky" who sounds like an escapee from Sgt. Pepper's Lonely Hearts Club Band.

Compared with the sensual streamlining of ELO's cosmic craft the junky flying-bedstead affair employed by the Intergalactic Touring Band for their concept set on Charisma, fails to exclude even the kitchen sink.

And the contents exemplify this finicky detail — some grandiose fragments of sci-fi rock complete with overture and epilogue, tell a tale of sorts.

Their five-piece band includes Ixol Phaane, actually Larry Fast, who bears responsibility for "computerised keyboard synthesis." And there's a galaxy of support: orchestration by Danny Beckerman and Wil Malone who wrote this Star Wars microcosm, also by Harry Rabinowitz and David Bedford.

And the cast list of singers includes Rod Argent, Arthur Brown, Dave Cousins, Annie Haslam, Ben E. King, Mr. Snips and Status Quo's Francis Rossi and Rick Parfett while Clarence Clemons of Springteen's E. Street Band gets a credit for possibly 20 seconds of sax soloing — get the idea?

Glossy booklet lists credits, plus the lyrics — many of them rendered in performance like heroin-hike Daleks — plus lurid comic-cuts illustrations. Not happy about this "concept" at all, though it may appeal to the 2001-watchers.

Themes

Less pretentious and therefore to a degree more acceptable, record producer Meco Monardo's "Music Inspired By Star Wars" (RCA) pulls across the horizon just a few weeks before the film epic hits Britain.

Pioneer of extended disco-stomp and the technology that produced hits like "Reach Out" and "Never Can Say Goodbye" for Gloria Gaynor, Meco has compiled one long take from a lot of the film's themes — all big-band brassy funk overlaid by Suzanne Ciani's space-bullet synth effects. Workmanlike side two features "Other Galactic Funk."

DAVE TRIES

September 30, 1978 SOUNDS Page 27
Electric Light Orchestra
Sweet Talkin' Woman
Their new single out this week
b/w 'Bluebird Is Dead'
Produced by Jeff Lynne
Jet Records
JET 121
First 250,000 in clear lilac vinyl

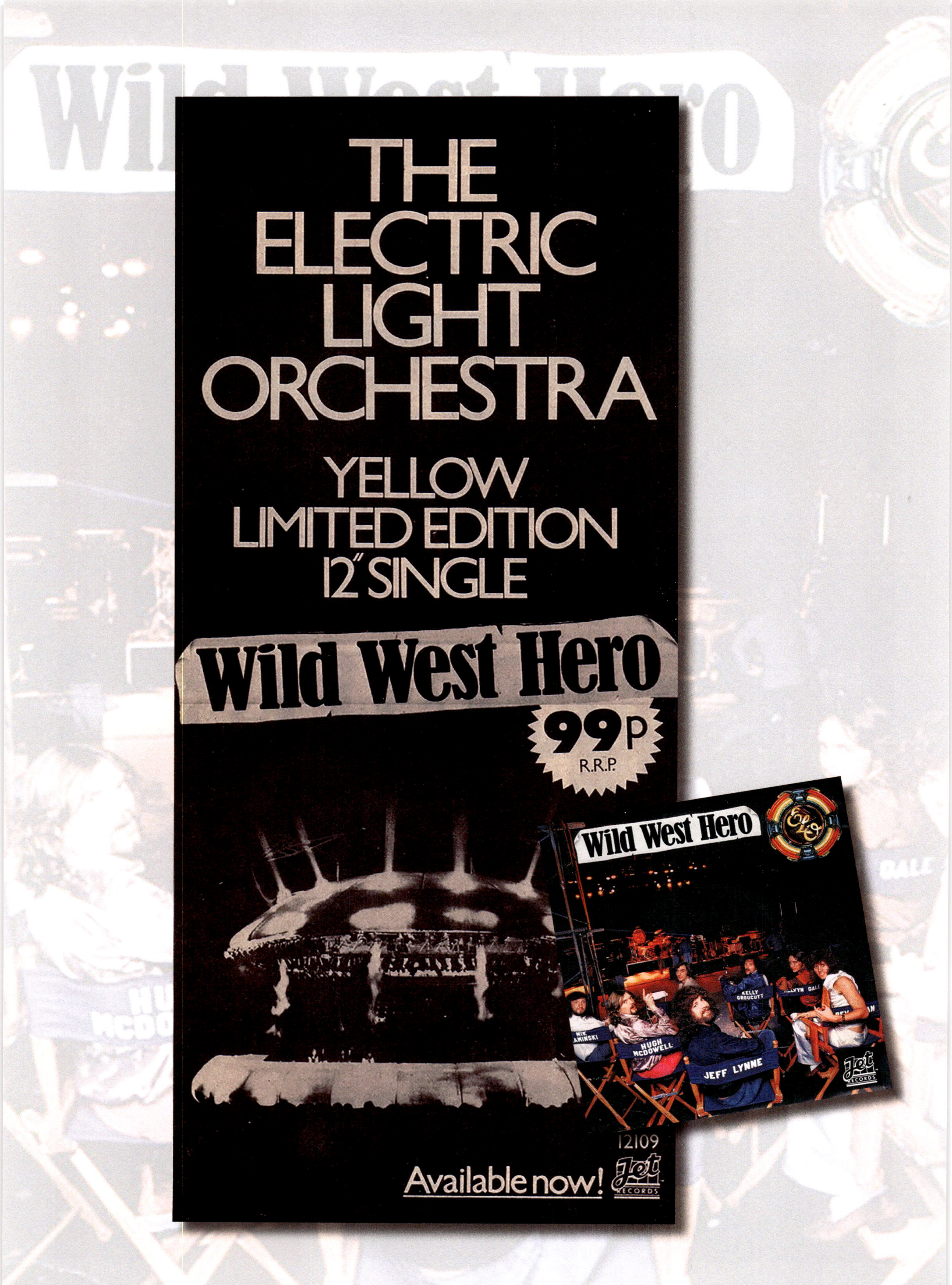
THE ELECTRIC LIGHT ORCHESTRA
YELLOW LIMITED EDITION 12" SINGLE
Wild West Hero
99p R.R.P.
12109
Available now!
Jet Records
Wild West Hero
HUGH McDOWELL
JEFF LYNNE
KELLY GROUCUTT

KELLY GROUCUTT

JEFF LYNNE

BEV BEVAN

HUGH McDOWELL

RICHARD TANDY

MIK KAMINSKI

MELVYN GALE

Close encounters with the Electric Light Orchestra

By STEVEN DAVEY

Wednesday evening a spaceship will land at the CNE Grandstand. But there won't be any aliens aboard when the cosmic oyster opens. The top of the UFO will rise, its lasers flashing into the night sky, and the mothership connection will be made with the Electric Light Orchestra.

The Grandstand spectacular is the third in the summer concert series Summer Pop '78. So far Toronto has witnessed those singing surfers the Beach Boys and English Mellotron rockers Genesis at the home of the Blue Jays. The $500,000 production the ELO will unveil is claimed to be the most elaborate and expensive rock stage production ever.

Drummer Bev Bevan of the ELO talked by phone from Omaha, Nebraska, about their upcoming Toronto date, on the opening night of the 44-date North American tour.

"I don't really want to give away all the technical details of our show because it will ruin the element of surprise for the audience. Because the space craft and the sound and light set-ups take three days to assemble, the tour is structured with A and B dates. Toronto is an A date and will probably be one of the biggest nights of the tour."

The Electric Light Orchestra's current world assault began in Australia in January, then hit Japan, New Zealand, and Hawaii. In June the band previewed the UFO with a week of concerts in London, England.

The British concerts left crowds and critics gaping. Music magazine Melody Maker burbled: "Honestly, when you find yourself actually applauding the stage at the end of a gig, then you suddenly realize that you've just witnessed a very special occasion."

The 60-foot space ship resembles the one used in the '50s sci-fi film The Day The Earth Stood Still. Instead of Michael Rennie on board, when the top lifts off, the Electric Light Orchestra will be in full flight. Ten lasers will shoot out of the craft's portals and form the ELO logo in light.

The ship is made out of fibre glass and aluminum alloy. Eight transport trucks move the entire set and NASA-uniformed crew of 45 assembles and dismantles it after each performance. A specially designed and constructed lightweight PA system is suspended from rigging over the space craft.

In recent years, as concert audiences have grown into throngs of tens of thousands, stage settings for these shows have become more and more extravagant. Alice Cooper and band were the first to use full theatrical sets, when they toured with scenery and props straight out of a horror movie.

The David Bowie show that played the O'Keefe Centre a few years back transformed the theatre's stage into a seedy London back street. The highlight of that show, coincidentally, was Bowie singing Space Oddity while descending from the ceiling over the audience in a space capsule.

David Bowie has since forgone the glamor route and now appears costume-less on a stark white stage under glaring neon light.

The Rolling Stones' tour before last featured a stage that resembled a lotus, complete with a floating sound system. During Star, Star a 15-foot inflatable phallus spewed confetti over Mick's crowd. At the July 4 date in Buffalo two weeks ago, the Stones' new stage set-up was a giant mouth 75 feet wide with the band playing on its protruding tongue.

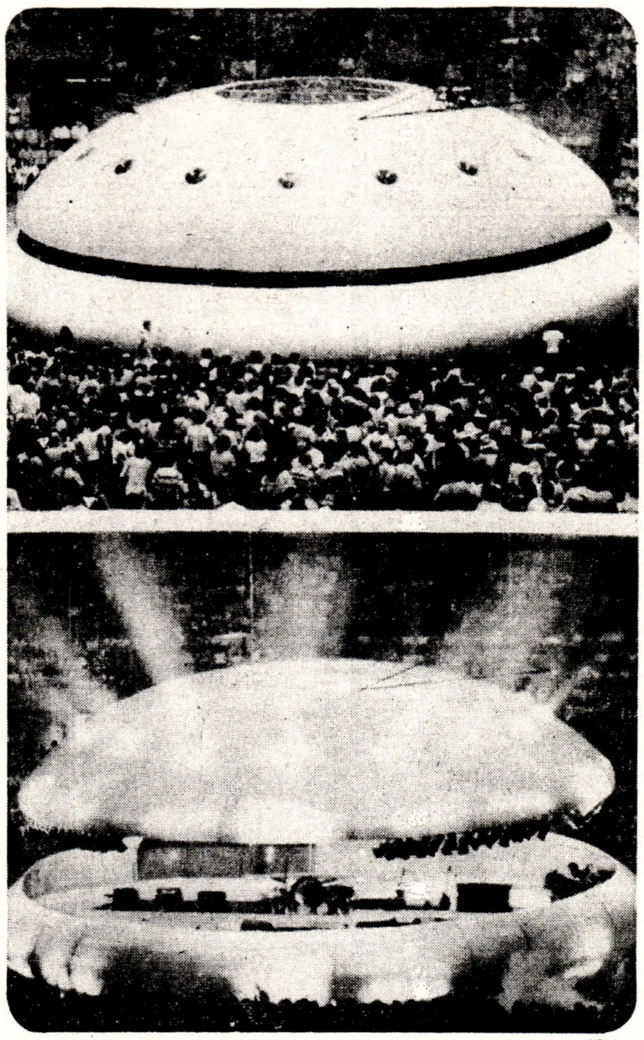

— UPI photo

THE MOST ELABORATE and expensive staging of a rock show ever is how the Electric Light Orchestra is billing its concert at CNE Wednesday night. The band will land in a flying saucer.

When The Electric Light Orchestra lands with its flying saucer Wednesday night, 75,000 fans are expected to encounter the third kind.

Opening the stadium show will be ELO protege band Trickster, and Meat Loaf. Mr. Loaf's album has recently gone platinum (sales of over 1 million units). The chubby singer has come a long way from his cult film appearance in The Rocky Horror Picture Show.

In the past year, Meat Loaf and company have risen from the El Mocambo to two sell-out dates at Massey Hall in April, and now to the big-time baseball park.

If you've found yourself mumbling the cosmic message from The Day The Earth Stood Still ("Klaatu barada nikto") or acting like Richard Dreyfuss in Close Encounters, making models of the Grandstand out of mashed potatoes, at the supper table, contact the Electric Light Orchestra, c/o UFO, CNE, Wednesday night at 7 p.m. May the Force be with you.

Electric Light Orchestra

ELO Comes to Town

By BRUCE MEYER
United Press International

For a while, a couple of years back, it looked like rock 'n' roll was going the way of P.T. Barnum, Florenz Ziegfield and Cecil B. DeMille.

Alice Cooper, Queen, Genesis, Kiss; the music ranged from the artiest to the crudest, but the search for bigger and better thrills seemed destined to turn rock into an updated version of the Busby-Berkeley musicals of the 20s.

Naturally, part of the audience eventually rebelled against all the glitter and the result was the New Wave, a return to the ultra-simple approach to rock 'n' roll.

But the best of the Big Show rockers are still going strong — and the shows seem to be getting better.

This year the Electric Light Orchestra has a production that's about as extravagant as they come.

Following a spaceship theme that has graced the covers of ELO's last three hit albums, the band — including its unique electrified string section — performs under a hovering flying saucer, a multi-ton affair replete with hundreds of lights and flashing lasers that lifts off the stage with a roar at the start of the show.

The ship is actually a rather fragile construction of gridwork and fiberglass, of course, lifted and suspended by a network of cables and pulleys. But it's a fine illusion, even if it provides the band's leaders, guitarist-singer Jeff Lynne and drummer Bev Bevan, with some anxious moments.

"You should try getting under that spaceship and wondering whether it's going to go up or not," says Lynne with a smile. "Sometimes it goes up and then it comes down again. Things get caught and the whole thing starts creaking and groaning and it feels like it's all going to break."

If the spaceship and the laser effects provide a spectacular frame for ELO's music, that music is still very much the point of the show. Since they formed ELO from the remains of the Move — one of the best, and least appreciated, British bands of the late 60s — Lynne and Bevan have consistently followed a uniquely innovative and highly successful line in rock.

But Lynne, who writes most of ELO's material, concedes that the original concept — a kind of rock 'n' roll chamber group — has evolved over the years.

"The first couple of ELO albums were a bit pretentious," he says. "We were trying to be something we weren't, musically.

"We were doing long, drawn-out songs," agrees Bevan, with a grin. "We were being clever just for the sake of being clever, putting in a really difficult riff with really strange timing, just so everybody would say, 'Oh, that's clever.'"

Whatever the band's self-criticism about the early years, the kinks have all been worked out now and ELO runs through its remarkable set like some kind of perpetual motion hit-making machine. The dense, powerful ELO sound is unmistakable.

"Half the sound we get is from the keyboards, but our live sound is the attack of the real strings mixed in with the synthesized keyboard strings. You get a very big sound that way," says Lynne.

Editor's Note: Electric Light Orchestra will play at Hirsh Coliseum Sept. 2. It doesn't look like they will bring their spaceship-stage, but they will have their laser show.

1978.
(Pictorial Press Ltd / Alamy Stock Photo)

Electric Light Orchestra Tries To Keep Its Members In Shadow

By Mikal Gilmore
RollingStone

With its 45-member road crew handling special effects as a 60-foot flying saucer and a huge laser show, Electric Light Orchestra is one of this summer's biggest concert draws, but the tour is hardly what you'd call dramatic or event-filled, like the Rolling Stones or Bruce Springsteen tours.

There is, instead, something obscure and anonymous about ELO. Few of the people who buy their records and attend their concerts would recognize the band's individual members on the street, much less associate the correct names.

"It seems like someone else who's famous and not us," says Jeff Lynne, the group's producer, guitarist and leader. "The ELO that's on tonight is the one that's famous, but it's just a group thing. There's no front man or face sticking out. That's what makes it easy for us."

Lynne sticks close to his band and crew members, seeming happiest when he's recruiting for an afternoon soccer bash, and looking pained whenever he's cornered in conversation by a stranger. In the past, he has refused interviews, passing the duty to drummer Bev Bevan, a naturally friendly and articulate man. This reluctance to speak publicly has made Lynne seem withdrawn and aloof.

"That stuff about me being a loner, it's a lot of rubbish," says Lynne after a St. Louis concert. His Brimingham, England, accent is so thick it verges on Scottish brogue. "I just like to do ordinary things. I like to be with me mates, and to do interviews. I just got to a point where I'd done miles too many and I've got nothin' to say anyway. I just wanted to do music really. I love the studio. I want to be in there all the time, but obviously I can't."

Maybe the greatest irony of ELO's success is that the man who named and conceived the group was the first to leave. Jeff Lynne hasn't spoken to Roy Wood, once his closest friend, since 1974. "We'd discussed having a group with strings so many times," says Lynne. "But we didn't work together very well at all. I don't think Roy wanted two leaders."

Wood was one of the founders of the Move, a group known mostly in England for smashing television sets on stage, dressing like Thirties' gangsters, getting sued by then Prime Minister Harold Wilson for character defamation and creating one of the most imaginative bodies of music that rock has produced. Bored with his own band, Idle Race, Lynne joined Wood in the Move in 1970 on the understanding they would use the profits to start the Electric Light Orchestra. Both were interested in creating a new rock sound with strings in the mode of the Beatles' *I Am the Walrus.*

ELO's first album, *No Answer*, was a fragmented affair, as was their first tour. Wood left in 1971 to found Wizzard, another attempt at an orchestral sound, while Lynne and drummer Bevan began recruiting symphony cellists and violinists for a scaled-down ensemble.

The Electric Light Orchestra: The seldom recognized faces behind the musical group.

Lynne has a keener ear than Wood for fusing electric and chamber ensemble instrumentation to a rock format, and was adept at redeeming ponderous overtures and interludes by segueing into some tuneful tracks. Lynne however now dismisses *ELO II* and *On the Third Day* as "pseudo-intellectual" and *Eldorado* (often rated their best album) as "overdone."

With 1975's *Face the Music*, Lynne garnered his first platinum album and finally assembled the band's current lineup: violinist Mik Kaminski, cellists Hugh McDowell and Melvyn Gale, keyboardist Richard Tandy, in addition to Lynne and Bevan.

Face the Music and the two subsequent albums — *New World Record* and *Out of the Blue* — are a casserole of Beatle allusions, classical puns and rigidly plotted pop arrangements, trimmed with Wagnerian string flourishes.

Photo Features Inc.

BEST LIVE SHOW:

1. ELO
2. Rolling Stones
3. Kiss

Jeff Lynne's Electric Light Orchestra swept the field here with thier spectacular $300,000 spaceship and solid-gold stage repertoire. Kiss, who took top honors in '77, dropped to third place this year, and Zeppelin and Yes, who came in second and third last year, were crowded out by the ever-amazing Rolling Stones, a forever-young fivesome if there ever was one.

EVENING STANDARD, THURSDAY, JUNE 1, 1978—13

ROCK SPECIAL: The band who surprised even themselves by their success

By James Johnson

Softly, softly into the super league

A MULTI-COLOURED 53ft object designed to look like a flying saucer, will be transported piece by piece to Wembley this week from the firm of ship builders in Bury St Edmunds.

It is to be one of the visual highlights in a series of concerts by the Electric Light Orchestra at the Wembley Empire Pool over the next couple of weeks. Every night for eight shows the spaceship will hover over the musicians before gently landing beside them on stage.

Princess Margaret, the Royal Family's occasional rock fan, was going to attend the opening concert tomorrow, but she has now dropped out through illness. However, around 60,000 of the group's fans will travel to Wembley for the shows.

Since all the tickets were sold-out within a few days, the concerts look as if they will prove how the Electric Light Orchestra have, quietly and unobtrusively, eased themselves into a position in the super-league of British groups.

"It's been a surprise to us," states guitarist Jeff Lynne, mildly. "The last time we played in London—two years ago—was at the New Victoria Theatre. We had trouble filling 3000 seats."

The group's success has depended on highly florrid, multi-layered music on top of a rock foundation. Classical overtones are supplied by the the two cellists and one violinist who all have a background in studying serious music.

Some critics have found the music reminiscent of the Beatles during their latter days and John Lennon is supposed to have said that if the group were still together they would now sound like the Electric Light Orchestra.

"I've heard he is supposed to have said that. I don't know whether it's true or not," said Lynne. "If he did say it, then of course I'm very flattered.

"The Beatles were an important influence on me, especially with their later stuff like Strawberry Fields and I Am The Walrus.

"Sometimes people say we sound like them when they're trying to be nasty. But I always treat it as a compliment."

While some rock musicians would embrace sudden success with unashamed excesses of one sort or another, Lynne is a somewhat timid individual whose main expenditure in recent years—like pop stars in the old days—has been to buy a house for his mother and father.

He would probably happily admit he is not the most charismatic figure to be found in rock music.

"I've seen him do interviews where all his answers were just Yes or No," said his publicity lady, a little glumly.

JEFF LYNNE

Record Mirror, December 2, 1978 15
The Electric Light Orchestra
Light Years Ahead
THREE LIGHT YEARS
NOW IN BLUE VINYL
Out Of The Blue
the double album
–12 months in the UK charts –
Tracks include:
'TURN TO STONE', 'MR BLUE SKY', 'WILD WEST HERO' and 'SWEET TALKIN' WOMAN'.
JETDP 400
CASS-JETCD 400
8-T-JETED 400
THREE LIGHT YEARS
– a special edition box set containing three complete ELO albums: 'ON THE THIRD DAY', 'ELDORADO', 'FACE THE MUSIC' and a special 12 page colour booklet.
Tracks include:
'EVIL WOMAN', 'STRANGE MAGIC', 'NIGHTRIDER', 'MA MA MA BELLE', 'HALL OF THE MOUNTAIN KING', 'DAYBREAKER', 'BOY BLUE', 'CAN'T GET IT OUT OF MY HEAD', 'POOR BOY'.
JETBX 1
R.R.P. £8.99
The Electric Light Orchestra's
New World Record
Tracks include:
'ROCKARIA', 'LIVIN' THING', 'TELEPHONE LINE', 'DO YA'.
JETLP 200
CASS-JETCA 200
8-T-JETET 200
©Jet Ltd. 1978

Pop

Empire Pool, Wembley

Electric Light Orchestra

TONY CURTIS, himself looking outstandingly dapper as the spotlight plucked him from the gloom somewhere near a strange, extra terrestrial object, announced to the Duke and Duchess of Gloucester last night that they were about to experience the "most outstanding rock group in the World today."

With that, and amid a colossal barrage of sound, a close encounter occurred as the saucer-shaped machine slowly parted to reveal an immense battery of lights above and the Electric Light Orchestra below, pumping away at their distinctive music to the accompaniment of a dozen darting laser beams.

It was a stunning opening. Not that the ideas were new: Queen and the Rolling Stones have used elaborate hydraulic stages to house their apparati, while The Who were dazzling audiences with multiple lasers many summers ago. But the combination at last night's charity concert was hugely effective.

Unfortunately the next half hour was a ghastly anti-climax of the most dispiriting kind. The sound was an horrendous jumble, the playing was uninspired — Hugh McDowell's cello solo did little to promote that instrument's further acceptance among the populace — and the initial impact of this important night for band and Invalid Children's Aid Association alike was all but lost.

Only after the drummer Bev Bevan made a disarming little speech thanking everyone for making them all so famous, did the group and their sound-crew come up with fare fit to lay before royalty and indeed, the less ardent followers among the 8,000 present.

"Strange Magic," a gentle, early ballad, provided the perfect link before a suite of up-tempo songs punched across with E L O's customary, but until then, untapped verve, and the thunderous climax of "Roll Over Beethoven," which brought the capacity house to its feet, the light show back in all its glory and the two mini-saucers scudding across the hall.

It remains a mystery why Jeff Lynne's group, so unsuccessful here two years ago that they could barely fill the New Victoria, can now play to eight full Empire Pools. The music is simple, heavily underscored with growling strings, and usually tuneful. They stage their shows lavishly. But there have been many greater nights at Wembley. J.C.

Nigel lights up the ELO

SCENE
with James Belsey

Nigel Gibbons in his Electric Light Orchestra tour jacket: "Sometimes I get fed up with world travel . . . I lose all sense of time and place".

BRISTOL'S Nigel Gibbons is the man who puts the light into the Electric Light Orchestra and other superstar bands.

He travels the world with mammoth rock shows as one of rock's top freelance lighting designers, and his customers include the Rolling Stones and millionaire American bands like Aerosmith.

Hundreds of thousands of fans saw his greatest triumph this year on the Electric Light Orchestra's world tour . . . the ELO's fantastic flying saucer stage creation.

Night after night, from California to Japan, his blazing finale of lasers, colours and effects won a standing ovation quite separate from the ELO's tumultuous reception.

Circus

At present he is taking a break from the larger-than-life rock music circus with his wife Sue and their three children.

They are moving home from Claremont Road, Bishopston, to Henbury, before he goes back on the road again. He rarely spends more than three months a year with his family.

He stumbled into the rock world by accident. Theatre was his passion when he first came to Bristol in the 1960's for a year's technical course at the Old Vic drama school.

He got a job as an assistant stage manager, then sound technician at the Theatre Royal in Bristol, leaving at the end of the 1972 season.

He met and married Sue, a Bristol girl working in the Theatre Royal's wardrobe department, and after quitting the Old Vic spent some months building flats in Kingsdown.

Deep purple

He said: "One day a friend I'd been at drama school with phoned me. He was the National Youth Theatre's technical director, and he wanted to start a lighting company."

The two set themselves up as a specialist service and their first customer were the Strawbs, who hired them for a major national tour.

"We did something horrific like 55 shows in 62 days, but it was the best possible training. By today's standards it was a pretty modest lighting rig, but things have got almost impossibly big now."

He went on to light a European tour by the Rolling Stones, and then Deep Purple signed him up as part of their staff.

When Purple disbanded, Nigel went freelance again and was soon approached by the Electric Light Orchestra.

They had just released their double album "Out of Blue" with its cover of a futuristic flying saucer. ELO's record company had commissioned one of this country's top stage equipment firms to build a replica of the spacecraft for their forthcoming world tour.

It was a daunting exercise, and Nigel was hired after the actual designs had been drawn up.

"We eventually built the white fibreglass saucer, 55 foot in diameter and with a complex series of hydraulics."

The saucer was first seen at the Empire Pool, Wembley, earlier this year. The 15,000-strong audience came into the huge hall to be confronted by what looked like a gigantic white hamburger nestling on the stage.

As the show began, lights played and colours flared, and the band were raised by a lift inside the saucer.

At the same time the roof of the saucer began to rise, revealing a huge battery of lamps and a brilliantly lit stage with the ELO coming into view. It caused a sensation.

The finale was even more effective, with ELO trooping offstage in a maelstrom of lighting . . . and then the loudspeakers played a lush minute or so of Benjamin Britten's "War Requiem" as the saucer's roof settled back into place. Every light in the stadium suddenly went off, a moment of total darkness and the house lights came up.

Nigel said: "The saucer is in California now, and there is a mad idea to dig a hole in the Arizona desert and leave it there.

Sue and Nigel stay in Bristol because they love the city. Nigel said: "Since I work overseas so much, where I live doesn't matter. I get tired flying day after day on tour. But the money's very good and the job's fascinating."

No spaceship

When the Electric Light Orchestra comes to the Twin Cities for its St. Paul Civic Center concert on Aug. 17, it will be arriving without the spaceship which the group has been using as part of its show.

The reason St. Paul won't get the spaceship is a matter of logistics, a spokesman for Magna Artists, the group's management company, said. The 60-foot ship, a replica of the spaceship that appears on the cover of the group's "Out of the Blue" album, will be used in Madison, Wis., on Aug. 16 and then be transported directly to Denver for a show on the 19th.

Since a crew of 45 requires 10 hours to assemble the $300,000 spaceship, there simply won't be enough time to bring it to St. Paul, the spokesman said.

The group, however, will provide a spectacular light show. An 80-channel light console for special effects will be used. Two portable generators will produce 525,000 watts of light needed for the show, which will be four times brighter than the average rock show.

Besides the lighting, four krypton and argon laser units will be used for additional effects.

The £96,000 home in the country . . . Cornerways at Rowington, a six bed-roomed house standing in four acres of land, bought by rock musician Bev Bevan.

Now Bev hits the 'mansion' scene...

by GARETH JONES

ROCK group drummer Bev Bevan has joined the growing band of pop stars who have bought mini-mansions in the Midlands.

He has paid £96,000 for a six-bedroomed country home in the Warwickshire village of Rowington.

Bev, who plays with the Electric Light Orchestra, is the second member of the group to buy a home in Warwickshire.

Two weeks ago Jeff Lynne, the group's vocalist, lead guitarist and pianist, bought Walsh Hall, a medieval country manor at Meriden, for more than £100,000.

Satisfactory

The agents, Stephen Viney and Company, of Harborne, who acted for both, today confirmed the latest purchase.

Cornerways, in Mill Lane, Rowington, was secured at an auction at The Forest Hotel in Dorridge.

The auctioneer, Mr. Peter Cariss, a partner with estate agents, Cecil Cariss and Son, said bidding started at £50,000 and quickly reached the final price after 20 bids.

"The price was very satisfactory. I expected it to realise more than £85,000. It is quite a high price for a property built in this century," he said.

The house, which stands in four acres of land, has excellent views of the Warwickshire countryside, said Mr. Cariss.

The Electric Light Orchestra is one of Britain's most successful groups and has vast earnings in America.

Other pop stars living in the Midlands include Roy Wood of Wizzard, who lives in Stourbridge, and Robert Plant and John Bonham of Led Zeppelin who both own farms near Kidderminster.

Rock star Bev Bevan, the new owner of Cornerways.

Jeff Lynne and Bev Bevan.
(Pictorial Press Ltd / Alamy Stock Photo)

Mik Kaminski, September 1978.
(Pictorial Press Ltd / Alamy Stock Photo)

HOHNER

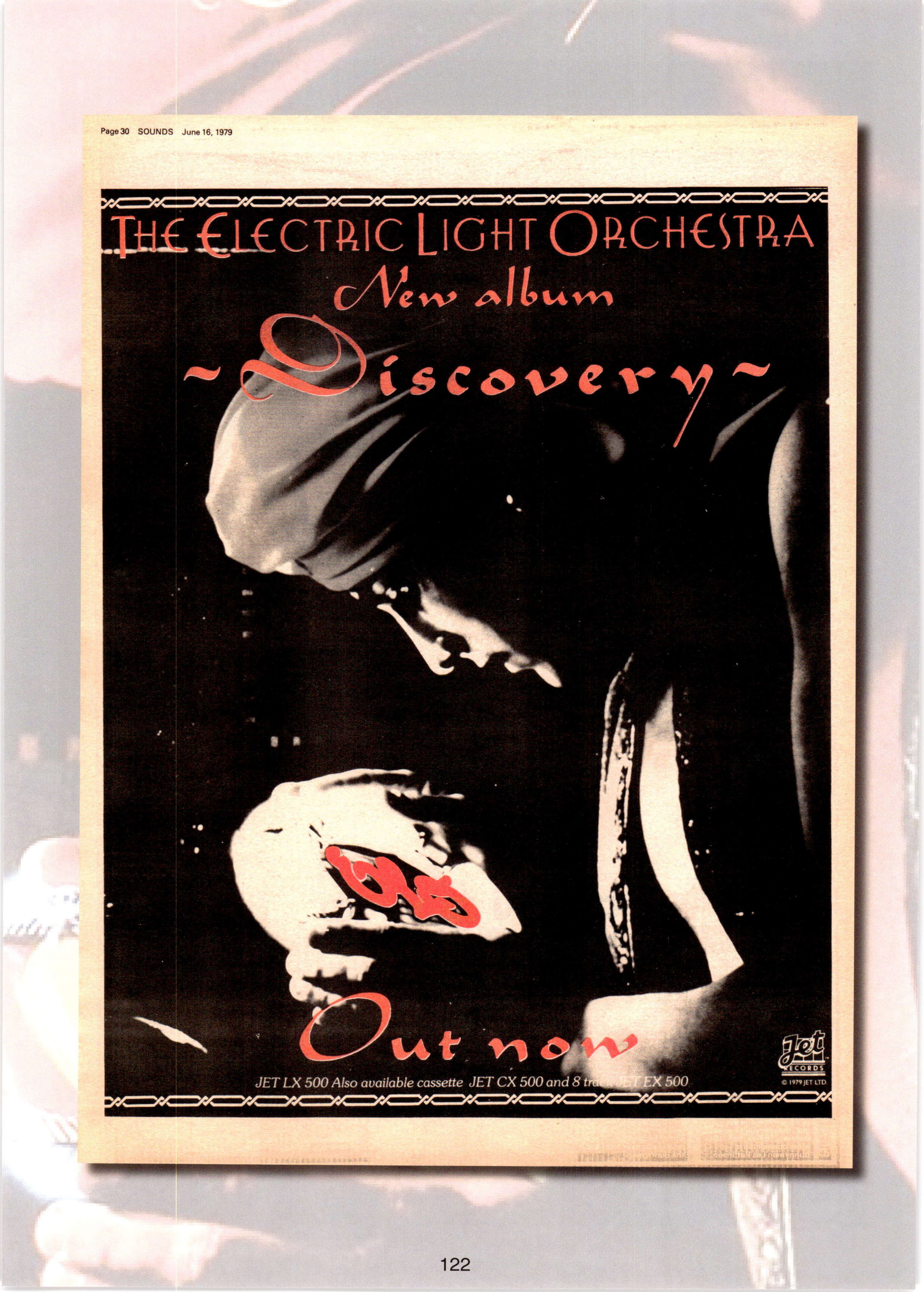
Page 30 SOUNDS June 16, 1979
THE ELECTRIC LIGHT ORCHESTRA
New album
~Discovery~
Out now
JET LX 500 Also available cassette JET CX 500 and 8 tra JET EX 500
Jet RECORDS
© 1979 JET LTD

For the promotion of *Out Of The Blue*, ELO embarked on an extensive nine-month world tour, encompassing an impressive ninety-two concert dates. Their enormous performance setup was nothing short of spectacular; it had an elaborate spaceship stage, complete with fog machines and a mesmerising laser display. The shows were billed as The Big Night. A staggering sixty-two-thousand fans attended the performance at Cleveland Stadium. Achieving remarkable success and popularity, the tour went on to become the highest-grossing live concert tour in music history up to that point. As part of the tour, the band also performed at London's Wembley Arena for eight consecutive sold-out nights, setting yet another record at the time.

Whilst on tour in Australia in early 1978, ELO was honoured with an impressive nine platinum awards in recognition of the outstanding sales achievements of both *Out Of The Blue* and *A New World Record*.

Recorded between March and April 1979 at Musicland Studios and released in the June, *Discovery* got to number one in the UK and Australia, and to number five in the US. As well as going multi-platinum in several countries both sides of the Atlantic, the album got within the top three of many such album charts.

Staying in the UK's number one spot for five weeks, *Discovery* hosted five hit songs in 'Shine A Little Love', 'Don't Bring Me Down', 'Last Train To London', 'Confusion' and 'The Diary Of Horace Wimp'. With many of the album's tracks having a strong — and very much of its time — disco influence, Richard Tandy went on to give it the nickname of Disco Very.

4 **Midland SOUNDS**

Paul Cole looks at one of the Midlands biggest success stories . . .

ELO

The Electric Light Orchestra, you might say, all started off with semolina pilchards climbing up the Eiffel Tower.

Rock mastermind, Roy Wood was greatly impressed by the Beatles' orchestral outings on tracks like "I Am The Walrus" and "Strawberry Fields Forever."

And being Roy Wood, he just had to take the idea a little further. A crazy dream was born — the perfect fusion of orchestra and rock band in one perfect working unit.

Jeff Lynne, hearing of the project, quit his legendary Idle Race and joined Ray and Bev Bevan in the last line-up of the marvellous Move — Birmingham's major contribution to rock'n'roll.

ELO was originally planned as a parallel project to the Move, and while the whole show was being put on the road, Move singles continued to flow — "Brontosaurus", "When Alice Comes Back to the Farm," "Chinatown," "Tonight" and "California Man."

Rock fans had the distinctly baffling sensation of deja vu, seeing first The Move and then ELO appearing on television.

It was in 1971 that ELO first emerged on record. The embryonic Electric Light Orchestra, bearded, shaded and mysterious, cut an experimental album of the same name — and produced on the way their first hit, "10538 Overture."

At this time the line-up was Roy Wood, Jeff Lynne, Bev Bevan, Rick Price, Hugh McDowell and any friends who happened to be around, like Richard Tandy.

Then, almost immediately in 1972, visionary Roy Wood quit, claiming that too much attention was being lavished on himself instead of the band as a whole.

Difficulties in getting ELO to work well live, and the frustration of the first chaotic — and catastrophic — performances did little for the Dream.

Roy formed the whacky Wizzard — a good time rock'n'roll band who produced classic singles — and took Rick and Hugh and him.

Jeff Lynne took a look at what was left, and with Bev Bevan, recruited himself on orchestra featuring musicians with classical or rock training, but rarely both.

"ELO II", issued in February 1973 was more controlled and featured the band's showstopper — an orchestrated version of Chuck Berry's "Roll Over Beethoven."

By the time the third album "On The Third Day" was released later that year, Hugh had returned from Wizzard and young Mik Kaminski had joined up — forming the basis of ELO as they are today.

"Showdown" — with its soul overtones, the best single yet — was culled from the album, and the superb "Eldorado" followed in 1974.

Bassist Michael De Albuquerque and cellist Mike Edwards left before the fifth album "Face The Music", and the line-up for ELO's second gold album was finalised — Jeff, Bev, Hugh, Mik, Richard Tandy, Melvyn Gale and Kelly Groucutt.

Hit singles like "Ma-Ma-Ma Belle" and "Evil Woman" followed and the sixth album "A New World Record" charted the course with songs like "Telephone Line."

ELO was now an independent high quality rock-pop band — the realisation of Roy Wood's dream — and the 1977 double set "Out Of The Blue" was the band's finest hour.

Now established as a major force in rock music, ELO developed a sound all of their own and became the best singles band since The Beatles.

The latest album "Discovery" goes even further as Jeff ever strives for new ideas with "The Diary Of Horace Wimp", one of the best pop singles ever made.

Gone is the chaos of the early days, and gone are the overly ambitious orchestral backdrops. ELO remain ELO — a truly original talent.

Mik's holiday for strings

When violinist Mik Kaminski burst forth with his own band Violinski, E.L.O. fans took a deep breath.

And when he wasn't even credited [illegible] E.L.O.'s smash "Discovery" album [illegible] worried fans took on frowns deeper [illegible] those of sad Horace Wimp.

Things looked ominous. Was [illegible] playing second fiddle to Jeff Lynne's [illegible] orchestral guests?

The answer was short and sw[illegible] Violinski album entitled "No Cause [illegible] Alarm", an official statement [illegible] record.

In fact Mik's solo excursion is [illegible] first of many by the members [illegible] Electric Light Orchestra.

Explains Mik: "All of us have [illegible] working on projects of our own, and [illegible] should be a lot of solo material [illegible] out in the future.

"My part-time band Violinski has [illegible] two singles out and we've toured [illegible] band in our own right.

Together

It doesn't mean that ELO are [illegible] way splitting up. After the massive [illegible] tour we did, we all wanted a bit of [illegible] off, and we all did a few things.

"I got together with some friends [illegible] we put Violinski together while Jeff was down in the studio getting all the tracks together for 'Discovery'.

"We're all delighted that everyone liked Violinski, and there'll be more to come while I'm not on the road with E.L.O."

Mik joined E.L.O. six years ago after answering an advert in Melody Maker — the traditional marketplace for top class musicians.

He arrived shortly after Roy Wood left Jeff and Bev Bevan and found things in comparative chaos.

"I answered the ad and was asked to go for an audition," Mik remembers. "When I got there I found this weird mixture of rock and the classics.

"It was all very very experimental when I joined and we all had a lot of really wild ideas. Nowadays things have calmed down a lot and ELO are a lot more conventional."

Pedigree

Mik's pedigree was anything but conventional. "I was about six years old and my granny was a violin teacher in Knaresborough.

"One day I picked her violin up and started sawing away on it. She saw that I had a bit of interest and started teaching me how to play properly.

"The result of that was that I ended up playing bass guitar at Butlins in Clacton. It wasn't exactly what I'd planned, but it meant money.

"I was standing there on stage peering at my sheet music to make sure I was getting all the notes right."

Mik later went to Leeds College of Music where he met new friends, formed a new band — and got thrown out.

"We were devoting more energy to the band than to the work," he smiles ruefully. "We were the only band apart from Curved Air who dared to use violin at that time, too."

And to ease any lasting doubts: "Mik, Hugh and Melvyn don't play on the albums, but they're essential and of the utmost importance for ELO on stage," say the band's management.

Lucky breaks right and left

ELO's Bev Bevan has something most big-name drummers lack — two broken wrists.

The right hand wrist was smashed in a soccer match; the left broken in a bicycle accident. Together they powered him to the dizzy heights of rock'n'roll success.

Bev Bevan's rise to fame took him from the small fun-time pop groups of the mid-sixties, to the giant rock supergroups of the seventies.

□

As drummer with Jeff Lynne's Electric Light Orchestra, he's idolised by thousands; as a Brummie born and bred he gets homesick easily.

Touring the major cities of the world has become routine, but he secretly prefers the close comfort of his £96,000 Rowington country house, and quiet dinners with wife Valerie.

But back to the wrists. Young Bev, soccer player of the month at Moseley Grammar School, started banging biscuit tins after watching his dad — a professional drummer in a smooth dance band.

And the broken wrists played their part: "They mean I have a unique style. No-one else holds their sticks the same way," he was to claim at the height of The Move's massive pop success.

A glittering new £35 drum kit later and Bev Bevan knew what the future held in store. At just 17 he joined Ronnie and the Renegades — a pop group which achieved overnight anonymity.

All he needed from then on was a pot of silver paint, some lucky breaks, and some devastatingly hard work.

Bev remembers it all today: "The first big group was Denny Laine and the Diplomats — all matching little silver suits and shoes.

"We couldn't get the silver shoes, so we had to buy new black ones and paint them all silver.

"The group was playing Beatles songs — that's what the fans wanted back in 1963 — and we had to get up and do requests. It was great fun."

□

But Denny soon left to form The Moody Blues — eventually ending up with Paul McCartney in Wings.

"We continued for a while, and then I joined Carl Wayne and the Vikings," remembers Bev. "We did the horrific German stint that the Beatles had done.

"We were playing 10 hours a night on weekdays, and seven hours a night at weekends. In between we had to do matinee performances — that was when the fun went out of it."

After the horrors of Germany Bev came home and met some strange individuals from other local bands. Clean-cut Roy Wood, Ace Kefford and Trevor Burton joined Carl and Bev on stage one night at the old Cedar Club.

"It was in 1966 and we all enjoyed it so much, we formed The Move. Just one year later we had the first hit with 'Night Of Fear' and suddenly it was the Big Time."

□

The Move grew to superstar status with a string of classic pop singles.

Jeff Lynne, leader of Birmingham's other main band Idle Race, eventually joined the fold with Rick Price, after the fond farewells of Carl, Trevor and Ace.

Remembers Bev: "We'd done the wild live shows; we'd had the hit singles; we'd done cabaret — what were we going to do next?"

Roy Wood and Jeff Lynne thought they knew the answer — an ambitious marriage of orchestra and pop group under the unlikely name of Electric Light Orchestra.

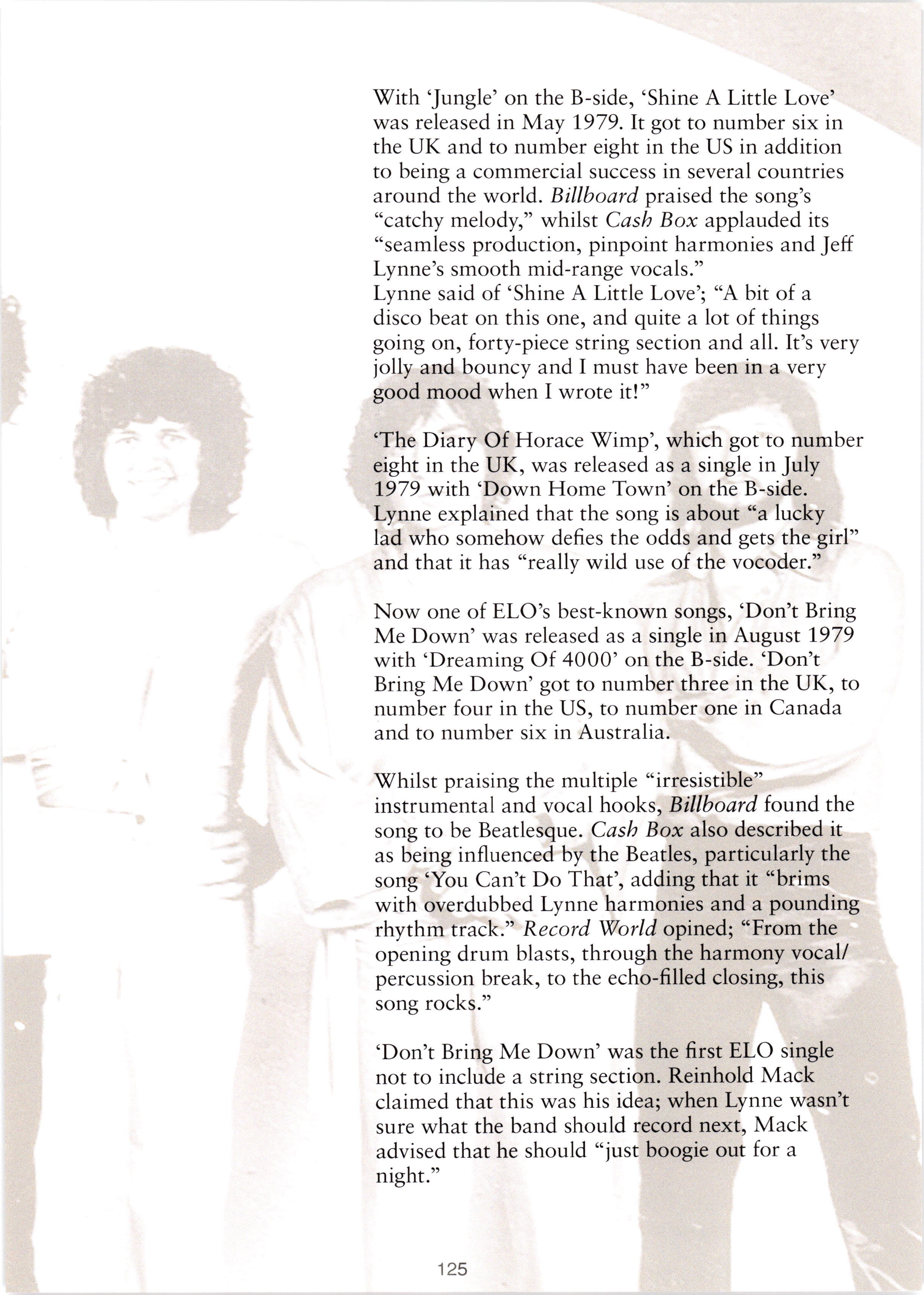

With 'Jungle' on the B-side, 'Shine A Little Love' was released in May 1979. It got to number six in the UK and to number eight in the US in addition to being a commercial success in several countries around the world. *Billboard* praised the song's "catchy melody," whilst *Cash Box* applauded its "seamless production, pinpoint harmonies and Jeff Lynne's smooth mid-range vocals."
Lynne said of 'Shine A Little Love'; "A bit of a disco beat on this one, and quite a lot of things going on, forty-piece string section and all. It's very jolly and bouncy and I must have been in a very good mood when I wrote it!"

'The Diary Of Horace Wimp', which got to number eight in the UK, was released as a single in July 1979 with 'Down Home Town' on the B-side. Lynne explained that the song is about "a lucky lad who somehow defies the odds and gets the girl" and that it has "really wild use of the vocoder."

Now one of ELO's best-known songs, 'Don't Bring Me Down' was released as a single in August 1979 with 'Dreaming Of 4000' on the B-side. 'Don't Bring Me Down' got to number three in the UK, to number four in the US, to number one in Canada and to number six in Australia.

Whilst praising the multiple "irresistible" instrumental and vocal hooks, *Billboard* found the song to be Beatlesque. *Cash Box* also described it as being influenced by the Beatles, particularly the song 'You Can't Do That', adding that it "brims with overdubbed Lynne harmonies and a pounding rhythm track." *Record World* opined; "From the opening drum blasts, through the harmony vocal/percussion break, to the echo-filled closing, this song rocks."

'Don't Bring Me Down' was the first ELO single not to include a string section. Reinhold Mack claimed that this was his idea; when Lynne wasn't sure what the band should record next, Mack advised that he should "just boogie out for a night."

SANDWELL EVENING MAIL, SATURDAY, JUNE 9, 1979 11

ROUNDABOUT — **The Pop Scene**

E.L.O. are down to a four piece — without their regular string players. It's the parting of the ways that was always in the air.

LEFT: Jeff Lynne with string men Mik Kaminski, Melvyn Gale and Hugh McDowell.

ELO left their regular string players out of the line-up on their new album "Discovery" and used instead a 40-piece orchestra and a 30-voice choir. POPeye writer PAUL COLE investigates.

RIGHT: ELO without strings (left to right) Kelly Groucutt, Jeff Lynne, Bev Bevan and Richard Tandy.

Pulling strings

But relax — it's only for the record. Mik Kaminski, Hugh McDowell and Melvyn Gale are absent with Jeff Lynne's permission on the band's new smash album.

Instead the Electric Light Orchestra project has moved another step forward The new "discovery" album features "special guests" — a 42 piece German Orchestra and 30-voice German male voice choir.

The nucleus of ELO — guitarist Jeff Lynne (who has just promised to marry his American girlfriend Sandi Karpelson), drummer Bev Bevan, keyboards wizard Richard Tandy and bassist Kelly Groucutt — have come up with their most commercial album yet.

And with Mik increasingly involved with Violinski, Hugh planning a solo album and Melvyn staying quiet, it's been made with a little help from their friends.

"We used a 42-piece orchestra comprised mainly of members of the Munich Philharmonic and an all-male German choir," said Jeff.

"It was on the Eldorado album in 1974 that we first used an actual orchestra rather than just over dubbing a few strings and it was twice as good as any of our previous albums."

The use of such grand orchestral power will inevitably lead to more frequent use of a term Jeff hates — "classical rock."

"People like to pigeonhole things" he said, "but I think our music borders a lot of styles. Mik on violin, and Melvyn and Hugh on cellos as classically trained.

"But we don't use that many traditional classical pieces, just a few familiar ones like Beethovens Fifth in Roll Over Beethoven."

The album's title "Discovery" was decided when ELO were thinking of the new musical area they want to explore — and there's even a little disco this time around.

"Quite often we don't know what a new album's going to be like until quite late on," revealed Mik Kaminski.

"Jeff will go into the studio with lots of ideas in his head and start about getting backing tracks down. He knows just how he is going to want things to sound.

"It's only when we hear his first tracks that we know what's happening. It's like listening to an album for the first time.

Mik's omission from ELO's new voyage of "Discovery" isn't as ominous as it first seems.

Despite the chart success of Violinski — the part time band he founded with life long friends, he's still very much part of ELO's future.

Bev Bevan, too, has long nursed ideas for a solo album. Three years ago he told me of ambitious wishes to record an LP of drum standards with friends like Led Zeppelin's John Bonham and Ringo Starr.

Mik, Hugh and Melvyn aren't even credited on the album cover — but do feature in a colour picture on the record's inner sleeve — in sight but out of sound.

And on sound, the clear message is that ELO are better than ever — and beating the best that most thought would be impossible to beat.

Mr. Blue, you did it right.

Now win ELO'S album

POPWORD has pulled off a real coup this week . . . you have read Paul Cole and Paul Walker's opinions of ELO's new album, Discovery . . . now you can win a copy for yourself.

All you have to do to win this very special POPWORD prize is to fill in the puzzle below.

Send your entries to POPWORD, Sandwell Evening Mail, 402 High Street, West Bromwich, to arrive not later than first post Wednesday.

The first five all-correct entries checked win an album each.

The editor's decision is final and no correspondence can be entered into.

Jeff's disco Discovery

FOLLOWING up the best album of 78, Out Of The Blue, which sold over nine million copies worldwide, cannot have been easy for ELO, writes PAUL WALKER.

But Jeff Lynne and his colleagues went back to their usual Munich studio and Discovery (Jet) is the result.

It has already spawned a stunning single hit, Shine A Little Love, and this opening track makes it clear that Lynne has started to "discover" disco.

I am still not sure that I like hearing Bee Gees style harmonies and high pitched voices as we get on a couple of tracks, but it's clear the ELO are to disco what the crown jewels are to plastic charm bracelets.

There is not a bad track on the album. The opener on side two, Last Train To London, must surely be the follow-up single, and Midnight Blue and On The Run are not far behind.

The Diary of Horace Wimp has Beatle-style storylines with some excellent work from the choir, while the final track, Don't Bring Me Down, shows the fans that they have not departed from their famed rock image.

Drummer Bev Bevan pounds away and the track is a real rockin' stunner.

POP PARADE — TONY JASPER WITH THE LATEST ROCK NEWS

ELO record another smash

THE ELO team is back with their first studio album since release of their amazingly successful double album Out Of The Blue, 18 months ago.

Discovery is the title, and the official release date is June 1. Advance orders for the album have reached 250,000, and it should replace Abba in the number one spot in the LP charts. The album comes packaged in a gatefold sleeve, and some say it is the most dynamic in content ever written by ELO's supremo Jeff Lynne.

Shine A Little Love is the first single from the LP and it is already charting. Flip side of the 45 is Jungle, taken from Out Of The Blue.

The last mentioned album has not been out of the LP charts for nearly 18 months. Also in the charts for ELO has been a boxed album set, Three Light Years.

Band leader Jeff Lynne comes from Birmingham and began his group days with a local band

After several invitations, he later joined The Move.

At the time, Move boffin Roy Wood was envisaging another band which would explore a mix of classical and rock.

ELO was born and with Wood contractually tied to Move, it was Jeff Lynne who eventually emerged in the driving seat, Wood eventually forming Wizzard.

Lynne along with former Move member Bev Bevan began making ELO into a major musical force, and assembled a group containing numerous classically trained musicians.

ELO mastermind, Jeff Lynne

In the song, there's a commonly misheard lyric where it sounds like Lynne is singing "Bruce" after the title line. However, he has since clarified across several interviews that he's actually singing a made-up word, "Groos", which some have suggested sounds similar to the German word "Gruß" (meaning "greeting"). Initially, unaware of the syllable's meaning, Lynne used "Groos" as a temporary placeholder to fill a gap in the lyrics. But once he learned the German meaning, he decided to keep it in the song. Interestingly, after the song's release, so many people had misinterpreted the word as "Bruce" that Lynne began to playfully sing it that way during live performances.

Reinhold Mack has a different recollection of how the term came about. According to him, Lynne was singing "Bruce" as a temporary line in a humorous reference to the number of Australian men with the name — ahead of an Australian tour. Eventually, they replaced it with "Gruss", which is based on the Bavarian greeting "Gruß Gott" (meaning "greet God").

'Confusion' was released in the UK as a double A-side single with 'Last Train To London'. It got to number eight. In the US, 'Confusion' was released with 'Poker' on the B-side and got to number thirty-seven. *Billboard* praised 'Confusion' for being "a superbly crafted single," describing it as "a mid-tempo rock track that mixes a Beatlesque sound with a hint of disco." *Cash Box* called it a "bubbly Lynne concoction, mixing glossy pop melody with alternately grandiose and circus-like keyboard fills." *Record World* considered the single to be a "mellifluous pop disc with the ever-present falsetto vocals and keyboard gymnastics."

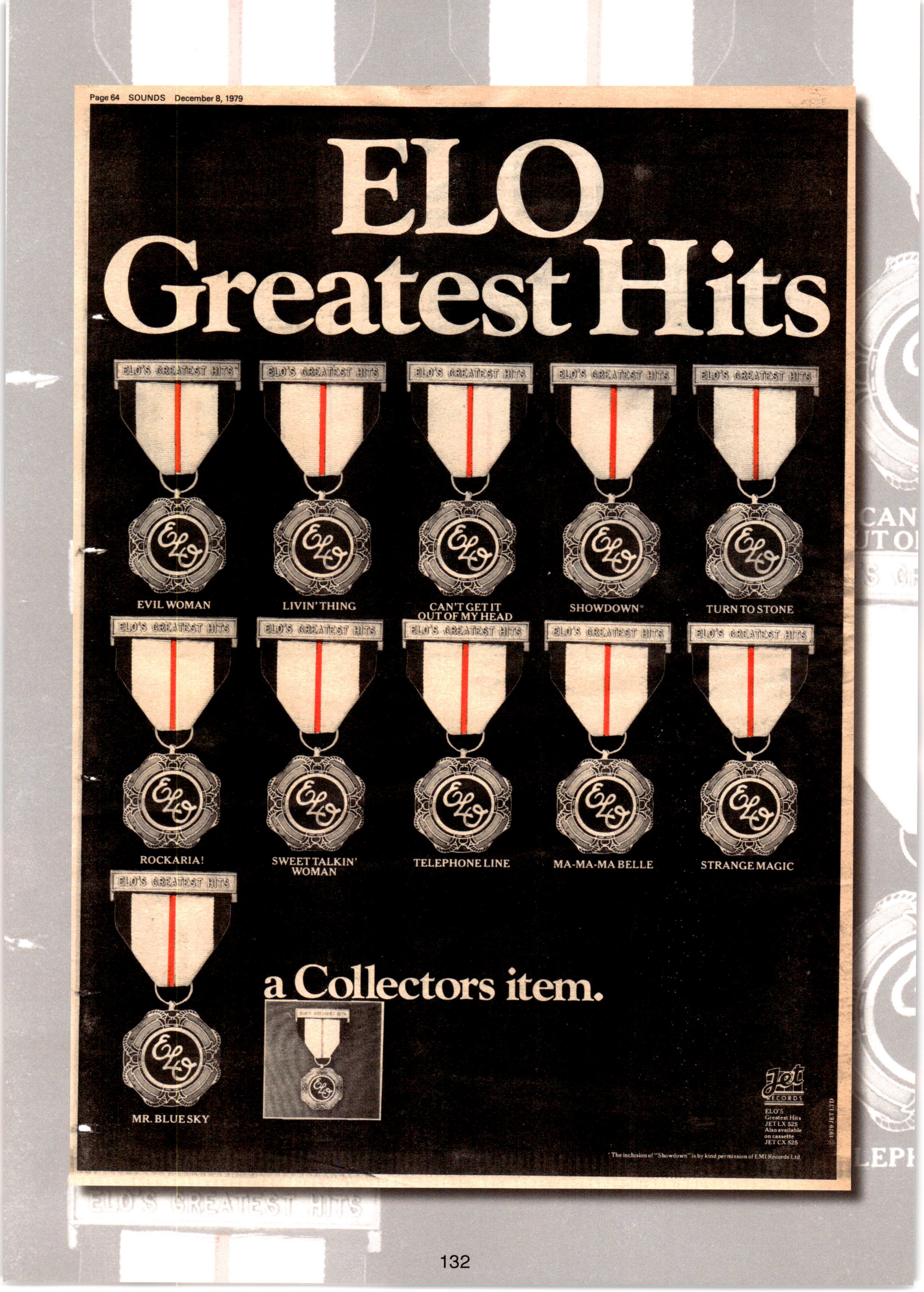
Page 64 SOUNDS December 8, 1979
ELO
Greatest Hits
EVIL WOMAN
LIVIN' THING
CAN'T GET IT OUT OF MY HEAD
SHOWDOWN*
TURN TO STONE
ROCKARIA!
SWEET TALKIN' WOMAN
TELEPHONE LINE
MA-MA-MA BELLE
STRANGE MAGIC
MR. BLUE SKY
ELO'S GREATEST HITS
a Collectors item.
Jet RECORDS
ELO'S
Greatest Hits
JET LX 525
Also available
on cassette
JET CX 525
© 1979 JET LTD
*The inclusion of "Showdown" is by kind permission of EMI Records Ltd.

Friday, September 14, 1979 Poughkeepsie Journal—17

Electric Light Orchestra deserves award

By Ken Paulson
Gannett News Service

Record review

ELECTRIC LIGHT ORCHESTRA: "Discovery" — Jet Records.

Any band that scores its first big hit with a rock version of Beethoven's Fifth Symphony and then grows progressively less pretensious deserves some sort of award for self-restraint.

The Electric Light Orchestra wouldn't have been blamed if it had followed the Beethoven-Berry blend of "Roll Over Beethoven" with a string of pop cantatas. Yet the band has succeeded by following the opposite route.

The Electric Light Orchestra is a singles band in the most complimentary sense. Their best LP's could have been greatest hits albums for most rock outfits. Each song stands on its own, a powerful package of pop delivered in less than four minutes.

"Showdown," from On the Third Day, set the pace for ELO's hit streak. Although the single never broke the Top 40, it did signal Jeff Lynne's maturation as a songwriter and commercial craftsman.

From that point on, ELO brought a touch of class to the popular airwaves: "Can't Get It Out of My Head," "Telephone Line," "Strange Magic," "Sweet Talkin' Woman," and "Evil Woman" were among recent ELO records gracing the Top 20.

Just when ELO seems to have explored every gimmick, Lynne comes up with a slightly different rhythm and irresistible riff. Discovery unveils nine new songs in that tradition.

"Shine A Little Love" already has gained national attention. The lyrics take a back seat to the wave of sound pushed forward by the hyperactive disco beat.

Even more impressive is "Don't Bring Me Down." ELO was formed by former members of the Move, a no-nonsense rock band known for its habit of chopping up television sets and home appliances in their stage act. ELO fell a bit short of recapturing their roots on the remake of "Do Ya" in 1977. On "Don't Bring Me Down," they eclipse the power of their early work. The least polished track on the album, it is also the most powerful — a rock attack propelled by a thundering drum beat.

The singles candidates don't end there. "Last Train to London," "On the Run" and "Confusion" all boast a fair share of hooks, with the latter recalling the style of the Walker Brothers.

There are some excesses here. The use of a 42-piece German orchestra and 30-voice all-male choir is a bit much for songs that are only slightly more sophisticated than those of Herman's Hermits.

"The Ballad of Horace Wimp" tries to be cute, but flounders with a case of terminal silliness. Weaker yet are the Bee Gees-influenced "Need Her Love" ("How Deep Is Your Love" revisited) and "Midnight Blue" (shades of "How Can You Mend a Broken Heart").

Still, the high points far outweigh the low, and even weak ELO is fairly listenable. "Discovery" is commercial creativity at its best.

Members of Electric Light Orchestra are from left Hugh McDowell, Richard Tandy, Kelly Groucutt, Jeff Lynne, Melvyn Gale, Mik Kaminski and Bev Bevan.

Rolling Stone

By Jim Farber

When Bev Bevan, the Electric Light Orchestra's drummer and mouthpiece, moved into his sprawling new mansion near Stratford-on-Avon in England, the trouble began. Local papers warned of a pop star moving into the neighborhood, while citizens circulated petitions to get rid of him. Property values were ready to topple. "They thought there would be pop festivals on the lawn and drug parties all the time," Bevan says. "Now they've gotten to know me and they see I'm quite a reasonable person."

Everything about ELO seems eminently reasonable — a model of blue-chip rock conseervatism. Over the last few years, ELO has become one of the more predictable best-selling bands, issuing a steady series of string-drenched pop tunes like "Telephone Line," from last year's double-platinum LP "Out of the Blue."

Along the way, ELO has acquired a pompous image, surrounding itself with such spectacles as a rising spaceship stage that looks like an intergalactic Whopper. ELO has had to rely on props to provide that image, since the band members themselves remain relatively anonymous. The feeling of impersonality is reinforced by ELO's thick, slick sound, which is continued (like any successful trademark) on "Discovery," the band's new Epic LP. Its single, "Don't Bring Me Down," is moving toward the Top 10, while the album is already platinum and selling like oil futures.

Bevan, 33, claims he himself is having problems with the bionic perfection of leader Jeff Lynne's production style. "I get bored with it, too." he admits. "In the studio, it's very restricting to work with this band, but it has to be done. I've tried doing more drum fills to liven it up, but when you put the orchestra and choir on top, it starts to sound a mess, so I have to keep it real simple. I've gotten to the stage where I don't even enjoy recording anymore. It's so mechanical."

On the business side, ELO is barely a band at all. Bevan and Lynne hold ELO's recording contract, and on the new album, the group has been trimmed down to just four pieces, with a 40-piece orchestra and 30-member choir glopped on top, cutting out the string section that tours with the band. "It must be weird to be in ELO — say, to be a member of the string section," Bevan says. "There's no real group feel about this band, except live. Then it's a real seven-man band. The strange thing is that Jeff and I don't really project that much onstage, and the string section shows a shows a lot of the personality.

Strings not mentioned

It seems strange that the string section wasn't even mentioned on the cover of "Discovery." "The guys in the string section were upset about it," Bevan apologizes. "I don't blame them. It's embarrassing for them."

One wonders, with ELO's corporate calm, if Bevan is ever nostalgic for the crazy, TV-set-smashing, effigy-burning antics of the Move — the mod Dadaist band in which he, Lynne, and Roy Wood got their start. "The Move went through so many changes that it wasn't a particularly pleasant band to be in, personalitywise. We actually got to the point of fist fights several times. I'm sure it showed through in the music."

As far as onstage violence goes, Bevan claims, "Our manager dreamed that up. I really had to act the part. It was never in me to be nasty to people."

Interestingly, an appreciation society for the Move and its offshoots — ELO and Roy Wood's Wizzard — called itself MELLOW, inadvertently predicting ELO's future. Still, as standardized as ELO's sound is, they've never lost their pop instincts, and it's only ELO's taste for the grandiose that has caused pop-loving New Wavers to overlook the band's finer moments. "The main thing, I think, is jealousy of our success," Bevan asserts.

"Resentment is built up by people. Real punk bands aren't going to like our music; I can understand that. But I can't understand why pop people wouldn't like us. People didn't resent the Beatles, and they were just a big pop group with a big production style."

Jeff Lynne plans to pursue "the big sound" even further by getting into some John Williams-style movie sound tracks. "He was originally asked to do 'Midnight Express,'" Bevan says. "And he's talking about some others now in Hollywood. It seems the obvious next step for him."

Page 56 SOUNDS July 19, 1980
THE MAGICAL SOUNDTRACK ALBUM FROM THE MUSICAL FANTASY OF ALL TIME!
XANADU
ELECTRIC LIGHT ORCHESTRA
OLIVIA NEWTON-JOHN
Xanadu – 1980's most spectacular album, featuring five dynamite tracks from ELO, including their hit single "I'm Alive," and five beautiful songs from Olivia Newton-John, including her latest hit "Xanadu."
XANADU
ELECTRIC LIGHT ORCHESTRA OLIVIA NEWTON-JOHN
Available only on Jet Records & Tapes
JET LX 526 JET CX 526
'XANADU' THE ORIGINAL MOTION PICTURE SOUNDTRACK

When released as a single in the US in January 1980, 'Last Train To London' got to number thirty-nine. It had 'Down Home Town' as the B-side. *Billboard* described 'Last Train To London' as having a "catchy pop melody with Beatlesque vocal qualities and a smooth layered sound." Comparing the song to Heatwave's 'Boogie Nights', *Cash Box* gave positive recognition to its "frothy pop melody" and "bouncy R&B-tinged rhythm line." *Record World* considered; "The electronic dance beat and lilting vocals are as timely as they are engaging."

In 1980, Jeff Lynne was invited to contribute songs for the soundtrack of the musical film, *Xanadu*. He wrote half of the songs, whilst the other half were penned by John Farrar and performed by the film's star, Olivia Newton-John. Although the movie itself didn't fare well at the box office, the soundtrack achieved remarkable success, eventually reaching double-platinum status.

The album produced hit singles for Newton-John, including 'Magic', which topped the charts in the US, and for Cliff Richard, who provided vocals alongside Newton-John on 'Suddenly'. ELO also had their share of hits with 'I'm Alive' (which earned a gold certification), 'All Over The World', and 'Don't Walk Away'. The title track, performed by both Olivia Newton-John and ELO, stands out as ELO's only song to reach number one in the UK. Bev Bevan later went on to say that whilst *Xanadu* wasn't one of his favourite records, he could appreciate how it managed to strike a chord with the record-buying public.

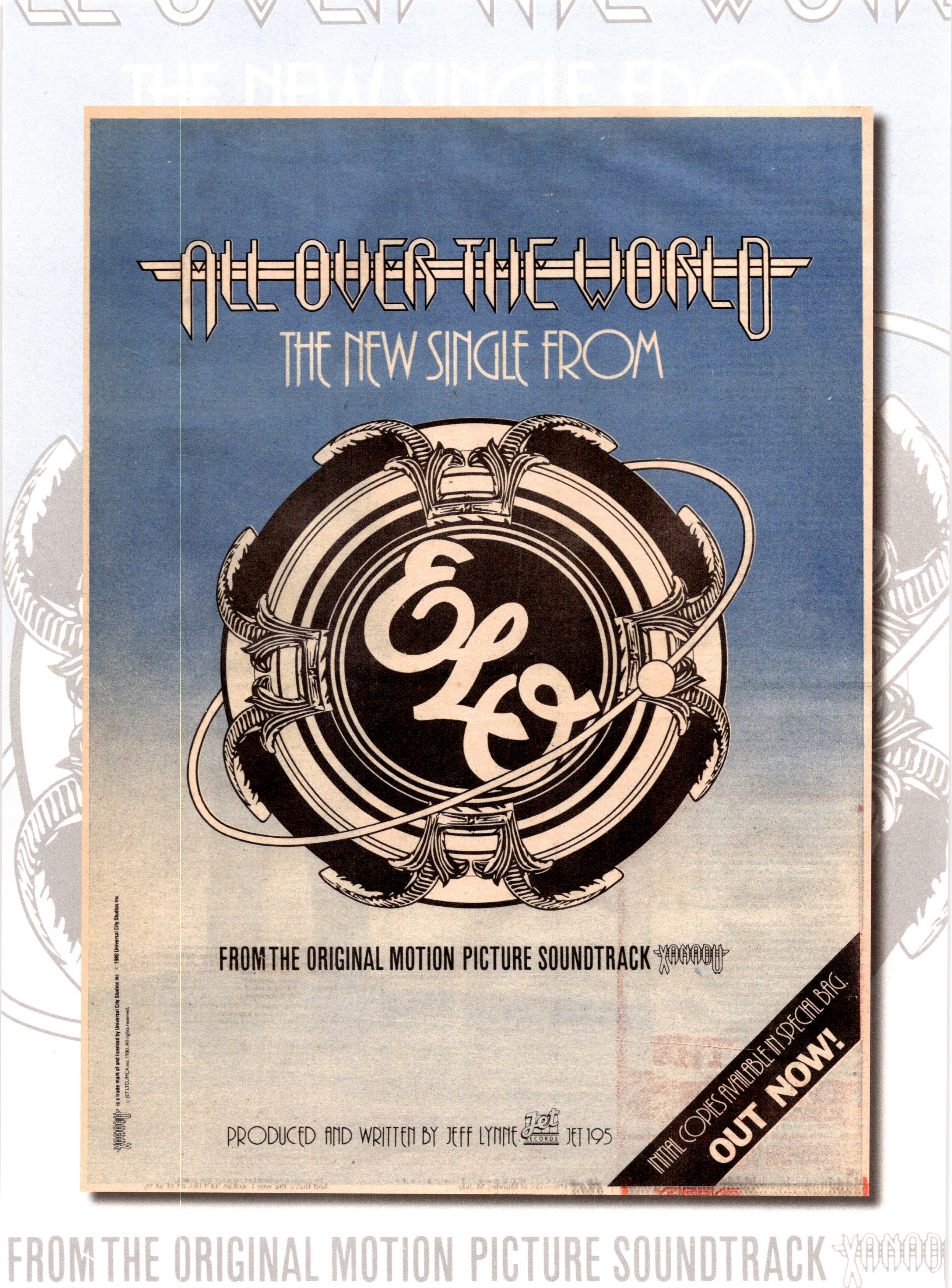
ALL OVER THE WORLD
THE NEW SINGLE FROM
ELO
FROM THE ORIGINAL MOTION PICTURE SOUNDTRACK XANADU
PRODUCED AND WRITTEN BY JEFF LYNNE JET RECORDS JET 195
INITIAL COPIES AVAILABLE IN SPECIAL BAG
OUT NOW!
XANADU is a trade mark of and licensed by Universal City Studios Inc © 1980 Universal City Studios Inc
© JET LTD./MCA inc. 1980. All rights reserved.
FROM THE ORIGINAL MOTION PICTURE SOUNDTRACK

In 1981, ELO underwent another transformation in their sound, which became evident on the July release of the science fiction concept album, *Time*. This album harked back to their earlier, more progressive rock records such as *Eldorado*. The departure of the string section marked a significant change in the band's approach, with synthesisers playing a prominent role, reflecting the prevailing trend in the broader music scene during that period. While some tracks on the album still feature studio strings (conducted by Rainer Pietsch), the overall musical landscape has a more electronic and futuristic quality in line with the album's theme.

As a concept album, *Time* is about a present-day man who is taken to the year 2095 and confronted by the dichotomy between technological advancement and a longing for past romance. Featuring a broad range of musical styles, the album got to number one in the UK and to number sixteen in the US. It also hosted the singles 'Hold On Tight', 'Twilight', 'Ticket To The Moon'/'Here Is The News', 'Rain Is Falling', and 'The Way Life's Meant To Be'.

Released in July 1981 with 'Time Stood Still' on the B-side, 'Hold On Tight' achieved great chart success, reaching the top ten in many countries. It secured the number one spot in Spain and Switzerland, took the second position in Germany, and reached fourth place in the UK. In the US, it got to number ten, marking the band's seventh top ten hit there. The song features a verse sung in French, which is a reprise of the first verse, conveying the message, "Hold on to your dream, Hold on to your dream, When you see your ship leaving, When you feel your heart breaking, Hold on to your dream."

Billboard heralded 'Hold On Tight' as an "affectionate tip-of-the-hat to fifties rock 'n' roll." *Record World* commented on the song's "rockabilly lead vocals, soaring Beach Boys harmonies, patented ELO keyboard waves" and commented that it signified "a good time for all."

'Twilight' tells the story of a man who falls asleep and then imagines everything that's going to happen in his life. The song was released as a single in late 1981 with 'Julie Don't Live Here' on the B-side. It got to number thirty in the UK and to number thirty-eight in the US. *Billboard* opined that it was "more intricate" than most ELO songs and that "a grand orchestral build coincides with swirling vocal harmonies for great effect."

'Ticket To The Moon' and 'Here Is The News' was released in the UK in late 1981 as a double A-side. It got to number twenty-four.

With 'Another Heart Breaks' on the B-side, 'Rain Is Falling' was released as a single in the US in January 1982. Although it didn't make an impact on the charts, *Billboard* considered it a "grand orchestral showcase in which Jeff Lynne showcases his vocal diversity." *Record World* noted how "celestial falsetto choruses introduce Jeff Lynne's childlike vocal lead" and that "swirling playful keyboards create a magical backdrop."

'The Way Life's Meant To Be' was released as a UK single in March 1982 with 'Wishing' on the B-side. 'The Way Life's Meant To Be' was the first song recorded for *Time* — it was done at Abba's Polar Studios in Stockholm, a few months before the main recording sessions took place in Germany's Musicland Studios.

For the promotion of *Time*, ELO embarked on a world tour that saw Mik Kaminski returning to the band on violin and keyboards. Additionally, Louis Clark (on synthesisers) and Dave Morgan (on guitar, keyboards, synthesisers and vocals) joined the onstage line-up.

Lynne's ambitions to follow up *Time* with a double album were thwarted by CBS. The record label believed that a double album might not fare well commercially and insisted on a single album. This led to the release of *Secret Messages* in June 1983.

ELO's tenth studio album, *Secret Messages* was recorded between December 1982 and February 1983. "We tried out a different place to record," said Lynne. "It was Wisseloord Studios in Hilversum, Holland. The sound of the room was just how I liked it. I enjoyed recording there so much."

The album was the last of ELO's to include Kelly Groucutt on bass, and Louis Clark on conducting duties with a full orchestra. Also, it was the last ELO album to be released on the Jet label. It got to number four in the UK and to number thirty-six in the US.

With 'After All' on the B-side, 'Rock 'n' Roll Is King' was released as a single in June 1983. It got to number thirteen in the UK and to number nineteen in the US, as well as performing well in several charts both sides of the Atlantic.

The album's title track — with 'Buildings Have Eyes' on the B-side — was released as a single in September 1983. It got to number forty-eight in the UK. With 'Letter From Spain' on the B-side, 'Four Little Diamonds' got to number eighty-four in the UK and to number eighty-six in the US.

With 'Train Of Gold' on the B-side, 'Stranger' was released as a single in the US in November 1983. Although it didn't make an impact on the chart, *Cash Box* considered it "a lovely McCartneyesque vocal and ballad about a small town boy anxiously facing the rest of the world, finding his first girl, and resolving never to return."

As well as being used for B-sides on singles, many of the leftover tracks from *Secret Messages* would go on to be included on the 1990 compilation boxset, *Afterglow*.

Following the release of *Secret Messages*, ELO didn't tour. Lynne — frustrated by declining audience numbers during the Time tour, CBS's decision to keep *Secret Messages* as a single disc, and conflicts with manager Don Arden — decided to disband ELO in late 1983.

Arden — real name Harry Levy — was arguably the most notorious music manager in the business. Having had his first success in the early sixties promoting tours, often involving the big American rock 'n' roll artists of the fifties, his first foray into management was with the equally-volatile Gene Vincent.

Probably because of his abrasive approach, Arden was more often than not successful with his signings, The Small Faces being one of his first big successes. An attempt by Robert Stigwood to take over management of The Small Faces saw the ugly side of Arden. Del Bromham of the band Stray, whose book *Rock and Roll Survivor* was published in 2022, recalled that Arden sent Wilf Pine (one-time Stray manager) and "Big Vinnie" to settle matters. Arden's henchmen grabbed Stigwood by the ankles and dangled him from the fourth-floor balcony window, threatening to let him fall. Victorious in his questionable methods, Arden built upon his reputation of threatening various forms of violence as a way of getting competitors off his back.

It was as a result of having signed The Move in 1968 that by default, Arden got ELO and helped to steer them to such a high level of success. However, not everything ran smoothly with his business affairs. In 2001, his daughter Sharon (who married Black Sabbath's Ozzy Osborne) told *The Guardian*, "The best lesson I ever had was watching him fuck his business up."

Generally, the musicians who he helped build careers for didn't see the ugly side of Arden; he was invariably making money from them. However, in an interview with author and biographer Jerry Bloom, Hugh McDowell opened up on Arden's nature and spoke of how the music mogul had pulled a gun on a concert promoter.

Following ELO's split, Bev Bevan went to play drums for Black Sabbath. As far back as 1972, in an interview with *Record Mirror*, he had expressed an interest in working with Tony Iommi — and not in the context of Black Sabbath! Bevan had mentioned being in discussion with fellow drummer John Bonham about the prospect of taking a supergroup on the road; one with the pair of them on drums, Iommi on lead guitar, Dave Walker and Robert Plant on vocals, Roy Wood on bass, and Jeff Lynne on piano!

Lynne moved into production work. Having already produced two tracks for Dave Edmunds' 1983 album, *Information*, he went on to produce six songs for the next one, *Riff Raff* (1984). Lynne also produced a song on the Everly Brothers reunion album, *EB 84*. Additionally, he wrote a song — 'One Way Love' — for former ABBA member Agnetha Fältskog to perform on her 1985 album, *Eyes Of A Woman*.

Under Lynne's name, Lynne and Richard Tandy collaborated on tracks for the 1984 movie soundtrack, *Electric Dreams*. However, Lynne still had a contractual obligation to create one more ELO album. As a result, during 1984 and 1985, Lynne, Bevan, and Tandy worked together as a three-piece, with occasional contributions from Christian Schneider on saxophone. Due to the absence of an official bass player, Lynne played bass. At both Compass Point Studios, Nassau, in the Bahamas, and Hartmann Digital Untertrubach in Germany, they recorded *Balance Of Power*, which was eventually released in early 1986 after some delays.

Although when released as a single, 'Calling America' (with 'Caught In A Trap' on the B-side) got to number twenty-eight in the UK and to number eighteen in the US, subsequent singles from the album ('So Serious' and 'Getting To The Point') failed to chart. Notably, *Balance Of Power* doesn't feature the use of classical strings. Instead, it has synthesisers played by Tandy and Lynne. Also, although they were working as a three-piece, a substantial portion of the album was created by Lynne, with Tandy and Bevan contributing their parts later in the process.

Balance Of Power got to number nine in the UK and to number forty-nine in the US. To promote it, ELO made TV appearances and played live performances in the UK and Europe. For this, with Lynne on lead vocals and electric guitar, the line-up was Bev Bevan on drums, Richard Tandy on keyboards, Louis Clark on keyboards, Mik Kaminski on violin and synthesiser, Dave Morgan on backing vocals, acoustic guitar, and vocoder, and Martin Smith on bass.

On 15th March 1986, ELO performed at the Heart Beat '86 charity concert organised by Bevan in the band's hometown of Birmingham. George Harrison appeared onstage during the encore, joining in the all-star jam of 'Johnny B. Goode'.

ELO's last performance for several years occurred on 13th July 1986 in Stuttgart, Germany, where they played as the opening act for Rod Stewart. With Lynne no longer under contractual obligation to commit to further performances, ELO effectively disbanded after that show. Following this, Lynne went on to work with George Harrison again; they produced an album, *Cloud Nine*, and then followed it up with *The Traveling Wilburys Vol. 1* (which features an all-star line-up of not only Harrison and Lynne, but Bob Dylan, Roy Orbison and Tom Petty). Lynne recalled how the idea for the band came about: "[George] said to me one night after we finished work and we were having a couple of bevvies, he said, 'You know what? Me and you should have a group'."

Also in 1986, the chickens came home to roost for Arden. He was arrested for kidnapping and torturing Jet Records' accountant Harshad Patel. Arden believed Patel had embezzled money from the business. Arden's son David appeared at the Old Bailey in 1986 for his role in the matter. Convicted, David Arden spent several months in an open prison. Don Arden was tried separately on related charges, but was acquitted.

In 1989, Bev Bevan, who co-owned the ELO name with Lynne, continued with a new project: ELO Part II. Initially, this group didn't include any other former ELO members, but it did feature ELO's principal orchestra conductor, Louis Clark. Bevan also brought in Eric Troyer, Pete Haycock, and Neil Lockwood. Their debut album, *Electric Light Orchestra Part Two*, was released in May 1991. Later, during their first tour that same year, Mik Kaminski, Kelly Groucutt, and Hugh McDowell — who were working in a group called OrKestra at the time — joined ELO Part II. Although McDowell didn't remain, Groucutt and Kaminski became full members of the band.

By 1994, after the exits of Haycock and Lockwood, the remaining five members, including their newest addition Phil Bates, released the album, *Moment Of Truth*. This line-up embarked on extensive tours until 1999. In 1999, Bevan retired from the band, and in 2000, he sold his share of the ELO name to Jeff Lynne. After Bevan had left what was ELO Part II, the remaining band members continued, calling themselves The Orchestra. In 2001, they released their debut album, *No Rewind*.

In 2000, Jeff Lynne marked his return with ELO by releasing a retrospective boxset, *Flashback*. It included three remastered CDs featuring tracks, out-takes, and unfinished works.

In 2001, *Zoom* was released. Although it was billed and marketed as an ELO album, the only returning member from the original ELO was Richard Tandy, who contributed to one track. *Zoom* features Ringo Starr and George Harrison as guest musicians. It got to number thirty-four in the UK and spawned two singles: 'Alright' and 'Moment In Paradise'.

Following the release of *Zoom*, Lynne reformed ELO with entirely new members — including his then girlfriend, singer and songwriter Rosie Vela, who had released her own album, *Zazu*, in 1986. He announced plans for an ELO tour. Tandy later rejoined the band for two live television performances. Alongside Lynne, Tandy and Vela, the new live ELO line-up featured Gregg Bissonette (on drums and backing vocals), Matt Bissonette (on bass guitar and backing vocals), Marc Mann (on guitars, keyboards and backing vocals), and Peggy Baldwin and Sarah O'Brien (both on cello). However, the tour that they'd planned to do did not go ahead.

Between 2001 and 2007, the reissue of ELO's catalogue was undertaken by Harvest and Epic/Legacy. The reissues not only feature remastered album tracks, but also include previously unreleased songs and outtakes. As part of this reissue campaign, two new singles were released. The first single, 'Surrender', got to number eighty-one in the UK. The second single released during this period was 'Latitude 88 North'.

In August 2010, Eagle Rock Entertainment put out a DVD compilation called *Live - The Early Years*. This compilation includes *Fusion - Live In London* from 1976, as well as a live performance at Brunel University in 1973, and appearances in 1974 on the German TV show, *Rockpalast* (which had not been released before). The artwork for *The Essential Electric Light Orchestra* was updated to have two different covers. The design used in the US and Australia was the same, while the rest of the world got the other design for a new double album release in October 2011.

Jeff Lynne at the Glastonbury Festival, 26th June 2016.
(Jonathan Short / Associated Press / Alamy Stock Photo)

Gibson

Richard Tandy and Jeff Lynne. Glastonbury, 26th June 2016.
(Jonathan Short / Associated Press / Alamy Stock Photo)

In October 2012, *Mr. Blue Sky: The Very Best Of Electric Light Orchestra* was released. This album features re-recordings of ELO's greatest hits, with Jeff Lynne as the exclusive performer. It also includes a new track, 'Point Of No Return'. The release coincided with Lynne's second solo album, *Long Wave*. Along with these albums, promotional cards announced the re-release of expanded and remastered versions of *Zoom* and Lynne's debut solo album, *Armchair Theatre*, originally released in 1990. The re-releases came out in April 2013 and have various bonus tracks. Additionally, a live album, *Electric Light Orchestra Live*, was released, featuring performances from the *Zoom* period. All three releases contain new studio recordings as bonus tracks.

On 12th November 2013, Jeff Lynne and Richard Tandy came together once more, performing as Jeff Lynne and Friends, where they played 'Livin' Thing' and 'Mr. Blue Sky' at the Children in Need Rocks concert held at the Hammersmith Eventim Apollo in London. They were accompanied by the BBC Concert Orchestra, with Chereene Allen leading on the violin.

Following the success of the Children in Need performance, BBC Radio Two DJ Chris Evans, with Jeff Lynne as his on-air guest, asked listeners if they wanted to see ELO in concert. This led to the quick sale of fifty-thousand tickets for BBC Radio Two's Festival in a Day at Hyde Park. For the concert, which took place on 14th September 2014, the band was billed as Jeff Lynne's ELO. It featured Lynne and Tandy, backed by the Take That/Gary Barlow band from the Children in Need concert, led by Mike Stevens, and the BBC Concert Orchestra. Lynne chose the band name in response to other ELO offshoots like ELO Part II and The Orchestra. Chereene Allen again played the lead violin. Lynne recalled; "We took a big chance. The crowd could've gone home any time, they didn't have to wait around for us at the end. But it was still full. I remember looking through a little gap in the curtain and going: 'They're still here!'." The success of the performance, enhanced by modern digital processing, led Lynne to consider doing a tour of the UK in 2015.

On 8th February 2015, Jeff Lynne's ELO performed at the Grammy Awards. During the show, they played a medley of 'Evil Woman' and 'Mr. Blue Sky' with Ed Sheeran, who admiringly introduced them as "a man and a band who I love".

In September 2015, it was revealed that a new ELO album would be released, this time under the name of Jeff Lynne's ELO. For this, the band had signed to Columbia Records. The album, *Alone In The Universe*, came out in November 2015. It marked the first ELO album of entirely new material since *Zoom* in 2001. The first track and single from the album, 'When I Was A Boy', was made available for streaming, and was accompanied by a music video.

To promote *Alone In The Universe*, Jeff Lynne's ELO embarked on a small tour, which included a full concert for BBC Radio Two, and two shows in the US — both of which sold out rapidly. The band also made US television appearances on *The Tonight Show Starring Jimmy Fallon*, *Jimmy Kimmel Live*, and *CBS This Morning*. In addition, a nineteen-date European tour was announced for 2016, with promise of a performance on the Pyramid Stage at the 2016 Glastonbury Festival.

In April 2017 (as ELO) Roy Wood, Jeff Lynne, Bev Bevan, and Richard Tandy were inducted into the Rock and Roll Hall of Fame.

Throughout 2018, Jeff Lynne's ELO continued to tour the US and Europe. Also that year, a video featuring the original recording of 'Mr. Blue Sky' was produced for the City of Birmingham. It was showcased during the closing ceremony of the Gold Coast 2018 Commonwealth Games as part of the presentation for Birmingham 2022.

On 3rd August 2018, a reissue of *Secret Messages* was released, presenting the title as Lynne's originally intended double album. It includes various tracks that were initially cut from the original release, such as 'Time After Time', 'Buildings Have Eyes', 'After All', 'Mandalay',

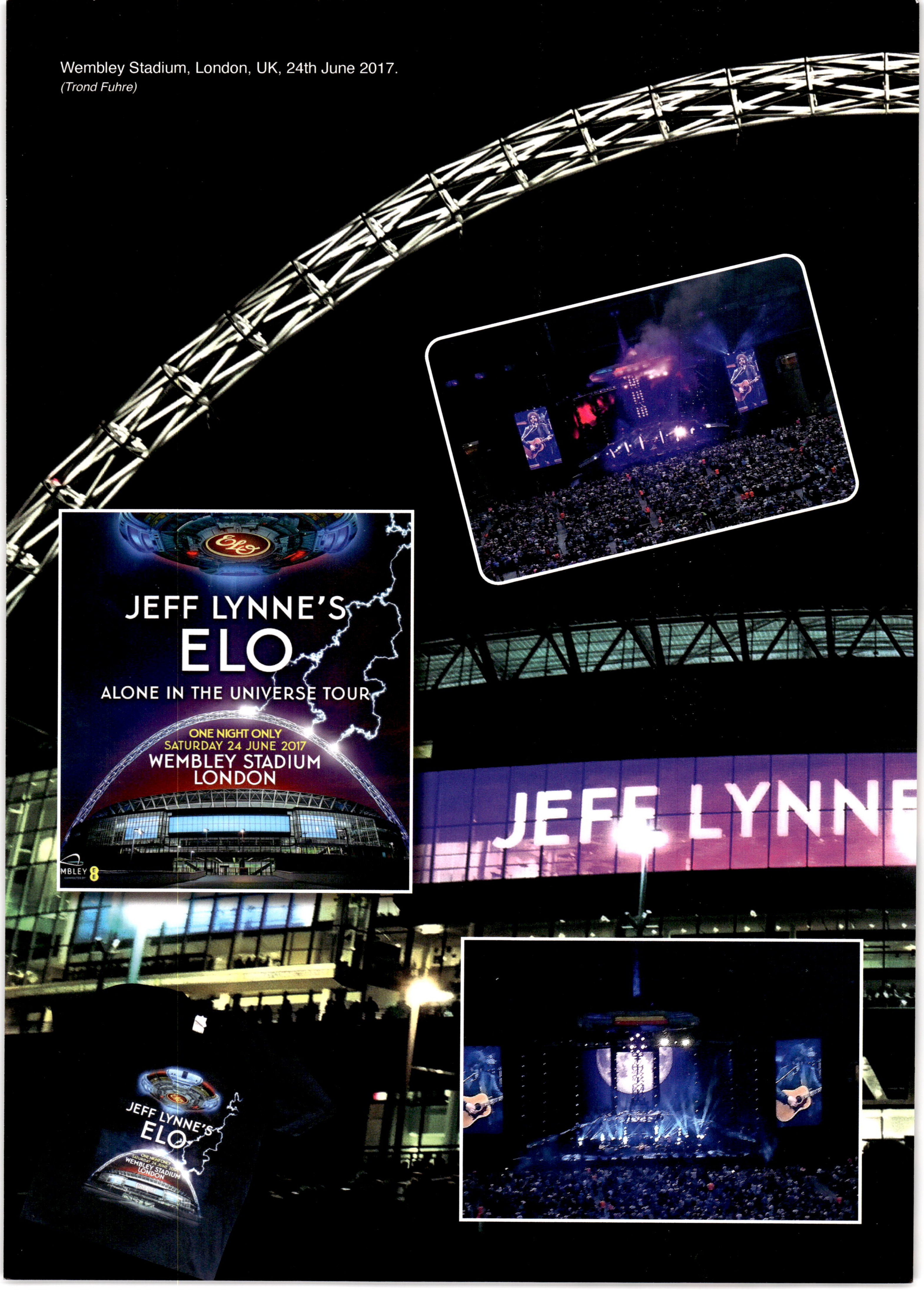

Wembley Stadium, London, UK, 24th June 2017.
(Trond Fuhre)

S ELO
LIVE NATION & SJM PRESENT
JEFF LYNNE'S ELO
ALONE IN THE UNIVERSE TOUR
SATURDAY JUNE 24TH 2017
GATES OPEN 16:15
ENTRANCE TURNSTILE N
BLOCK A6
ROW N
SEAT
WEMBLEY CONNECTED BY EE
DOWNLOAD THE APP
inspiring · memories
PORTER/ROBERT
28-21753
BK A6 ROW N SEAT
TURNSTILE N
110.00

Jeff Lynne's ELO performing at
Oslo's Spektrum,
14th September 2018.
(Terje Dokken / Gonzales Photo / Alamy Stock Photo)

Spektrum, Oslo,
14th September 2018.
(Terje Dokken / Gonzales Photo / Alamy Stock Photo)

‘Hello My Old Friend’, ‘Endless Lies’, and ‘No Way Out’. “This will be the first time *Secret Messages* has escaped intact,” said Lynne. “Thanks to all you great fans who’ve been asking to hear the original double album for a very long time.”

Having toured the US in summer 2019, in the November, Jeff Lynne’s ELO released *From Out Of Nowhere*. The album got to number one in the UK and to number forty-seven in the US. The title track and ‘Time Of Our Life’ were released as singles. Although a tour had been announced, sadly, due to the COVID-19 pandemic, it wasn’t to be. Still though, overall, the last few years have been a triumph for Lynne and the ELO legacy. “I think I’m most proud of the fact that I’m still out there doing it,” he said. “I haven’t packed it in yet, because I still love it. You can’t ask for more than that.” Indeed, at the time of writing this book, Jeff Lynne’s ELO is due to tour the US between August and October 2024. Billed as the Over And Out Tour, it has been announced as a final tour of that part of the world.

Across a tenure spanning over five decades, through various line-ups of raw and unabridged talent, ELO’s music has left an indelible mark on the hearts and minds of people around the world. With their harmonious blend of rock, pop, and orchestral elements, the band have transcended genres and styles, delivering a sound that is timeless, fun, and widely appealing. It’s a testament to ELO’s enduring legacy that their melodies continue to inspire and uplift new generations. In celebration of the brilliance of ELO’s innovation, it’s plausible that their music will live on, touching the lives of many more, for years to come.

Members

Jeff Lynne - lead and backing vocals, guitars, bass, piano, keyboards, cello, drums, percussion (1970-1986, 2000-2001, 2014-present)

Richard Tandy - piano, keyboards, synthesiser, bass, guitar, backing vocals (1971-1986, 2000-2001, 2014-2016) (died 2024)

Bev Bevan - drums, percussion, backing vocals (1970-1986)

Bill Hunt - French horn, keyboard (1970-1972)

Roy Wood - lead and backing vocals, guitars, bass, cello, oboe, bassoon (1970-1972)

Steve Woolam - violin (1970-1971) (died 1971)

Mike Edwards - cello (1971-1974) (died 2010)

Hugh McDowell - cello (1971-1972, 1973-1979) (died 2018)

Wilfred Gibson - violin (1971-1973) (died 2014)

Mike de Albuquerque - bass, backing vocals (1972-1974)

Colin Walker - cello (1972-1973)

Mik Kaminski - violin (1973-1979)

Kelly Groucutt - bass, lead and backing vocals (1974-1983) (died 2009)

Melvyn Gale - cello (1974-1979)

THE ELECTRIC LIGHT ORCHESTRA
THE ELECTRIC LIGHT ORCHESTRA
ON THE THIRD DAY
ELECTRIC LIGHT ORCHESTRA
Eldorado
Electric Light Orchestra
FACE THE MUSIC
Electric Light Orchestra
A NEW WORLD RECORD
Electric Light Orchestra
Out of the Blue
ELECTRIC LIGHT ORCHESTRA
Discovery
FROM THE ORIGINAL MOTION PICTURE SOUNDTRACK
XANADU
ELECTRIC LIGHT ORCHESTRA
OLIVIA NEWTON-JOHN
TIME
ELECTRIC LIGHT ORCHESTRA
SECRET MESSAGES
ELECTRIC LIGHT ORCHESTRA • BALANCE OF POWER
ELECTRIC LIGHT ORCHESTRA
ZOOM
JEFF LYNNE'S ELO
ALONE IN THE UNIVERSE
JEFF LYNNE'S ELO
FROM OUT OF NOWHERE

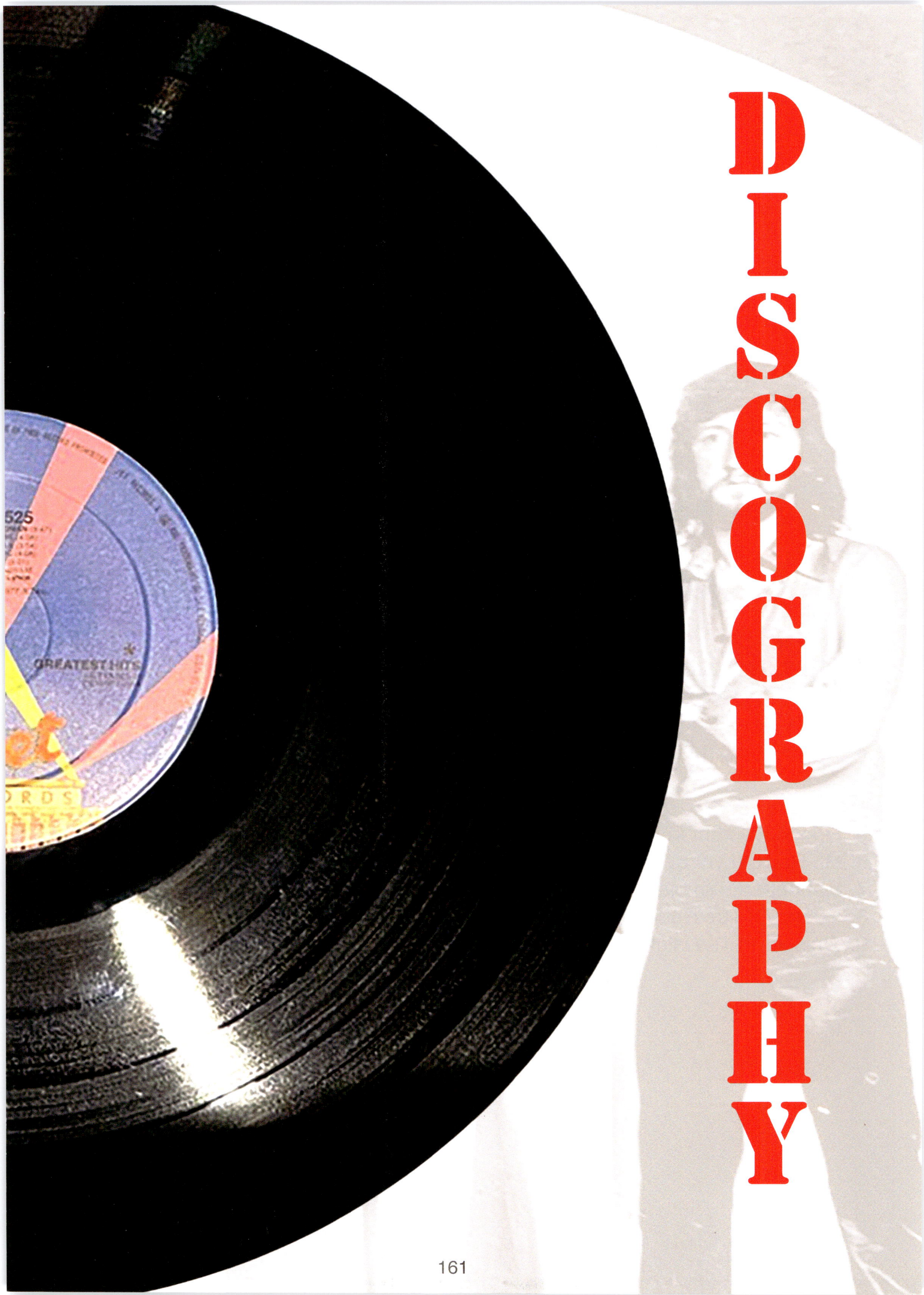

DISCOGRAPHY

The Electric Light Orchestra (1971)

Side One

1. 10538 Overture (Jeff Lynne) (5:32)
2. Look At Me Now (Roy Wood) (3:17)
3. Nellie Takes Her Bow (Lynne) (5:59)
4. The Battle Of Marston Moor (July 2nd 1644) (Wood) (6:03)

Side Two

5. First Movement (Jumping Biz) (Wood) (3:00)
6. Mr. Radio (Lynne) (5:04)
7. Manhattan Rumble (49th Street Massacre) (Lynne) (4:22)
8. Queen Of The Hours (Lynne) (3:22)
9. Whisper In The Night (Wood) (4:50)

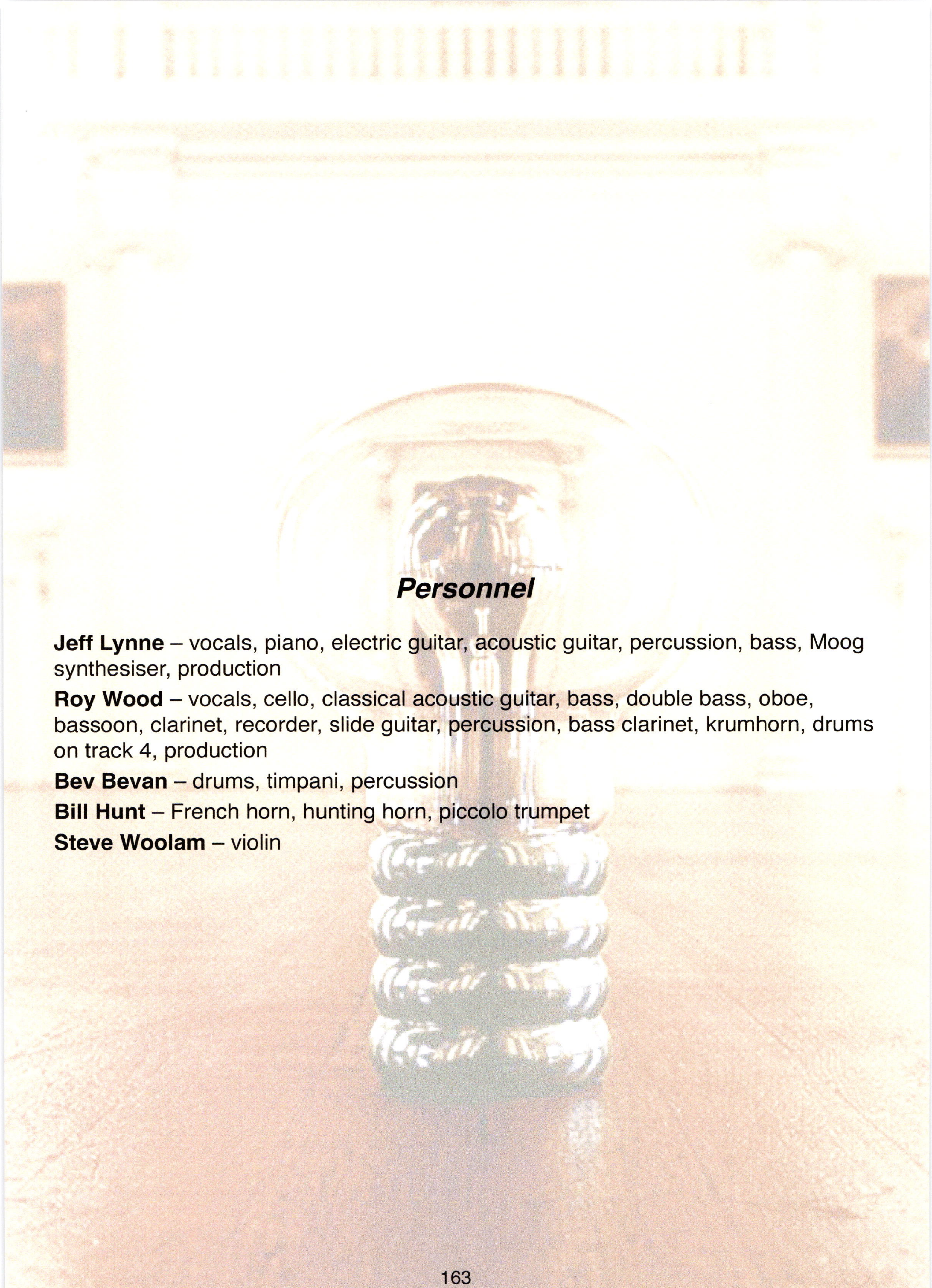

Personnel

Jeff Lynne – vocals, piano, electric guitar, acoustic guitar, percussion, bass, Moog synthesiser, production

Roy Wood – vocals, cello, classical acoustic guitar, bass, double bass, oboe, bassoon, clarinet, recorder, slide guitar, percussion, bass clarinet, krumhorn, drums on track 4, production

Bev Bevan – drums, timpani, percussion

Bill Hunt – French horn, hunting horn, piccolo trumpet

Steve Woolam – violin

ELO 2 (1973)

All tracks written by Jeff Lynne, except where noted

Side One
1. In Old England Town (Boogie No. 2) (6:56)
2. Momma (retitled 'Mama' on US edition) (7:03)
3. Roll Over Beethoven (Chuck Berry, Ludwig van Beethoven) (7:03 UK and Japanese releases) (8:09)

Side Two
4. From The Sun To The World (Boogie No. 1) (8:20)
5. Kuiama (11:19)

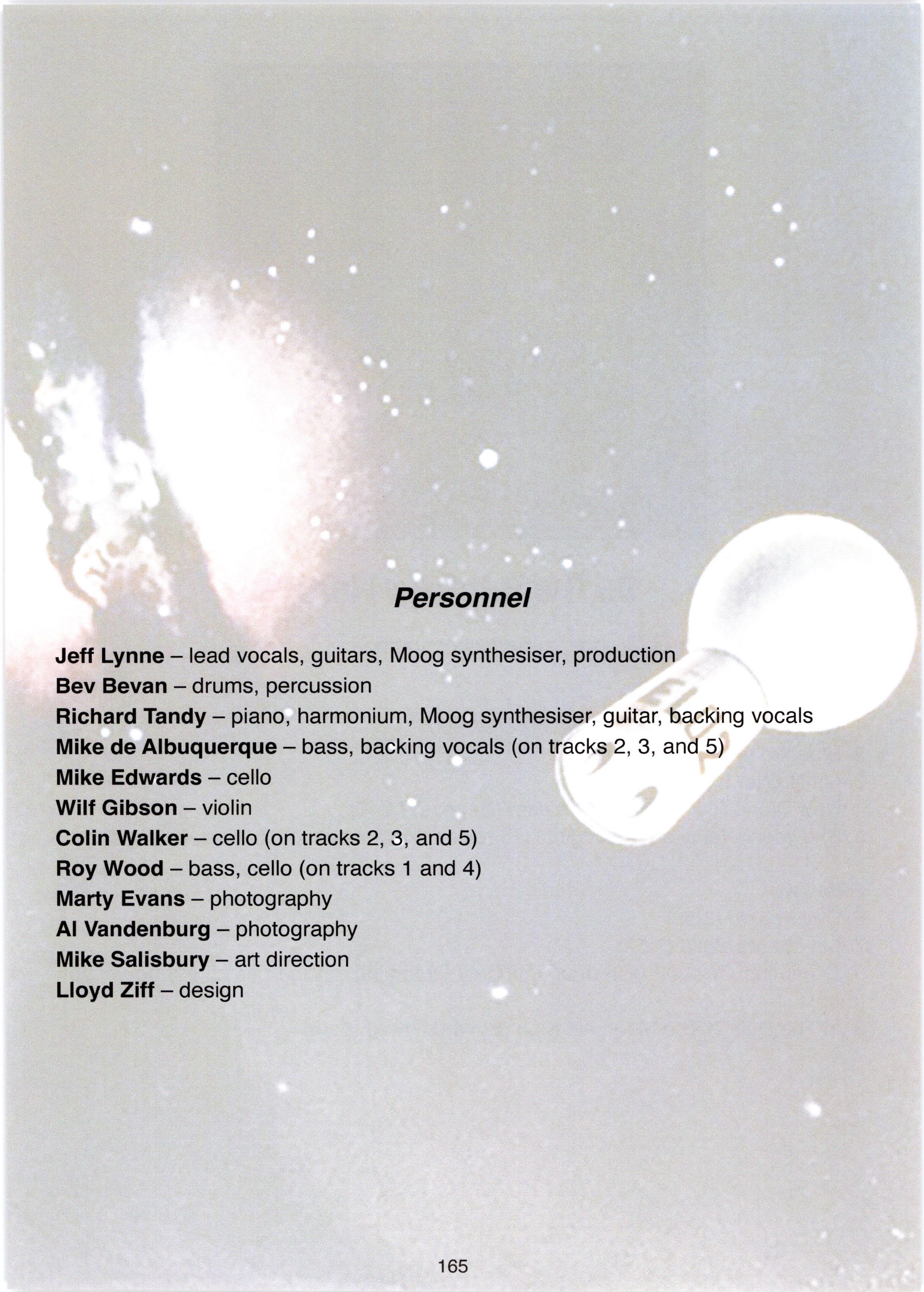

Personnel

Jeff Lynne – lead vocals, guitars, Moog synthesiser, production
Bev Bevan – drums, percussion
Richard Tandy – piano, harmonium, Moog synthesiser, guitar, backing vocals
Mike de Albuquerque – bass, backing vocals (on tracks 2, 3, and 5)
Mike Edwards – cello
Wilf Gibson – violin
Colin Walker – cello (on tracks 2, 3, and 5)
Roy Wood – bass, cello (on tracks 1 and 4)
Marty Evans – photography
Al Vandenburg – photography
Mike Salisbury – art direction
Lloyd Ziff – design

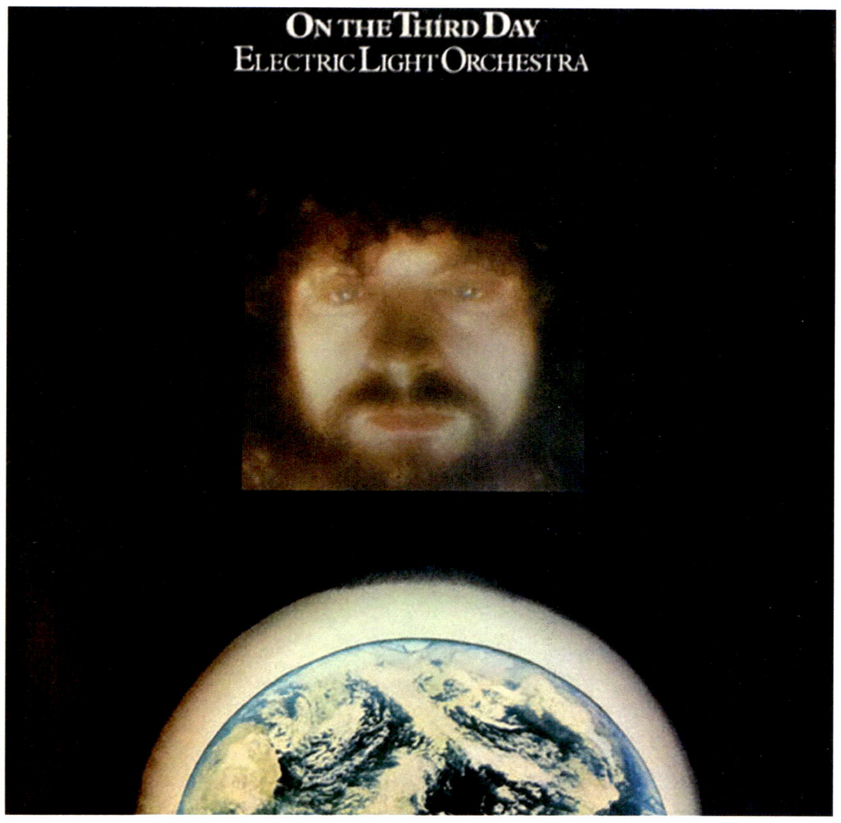

On The Third Day (1973)

All tracks written by Jeff Lynne, except where noted

Side One
1. Ocean Breakup/King Of The Universe (4:05)
2. Bluebird Is Dead (4:25)
3. Oh No Not Susan (2:52)
4. New World Rising/Ocean Breakup (Reprise) (4:40)
5. Showdown (only on the original US release and subsequent reissues) (4:15)

Side Two
6. Daybreaker (3:50)
7. Ma-Ma-Ma Belle (3:52)
8. Dreaming Of 4000 (listed as 'I'm Only Dreaming' on the cassette tape version (5:00)
9. In The Hall Of The Mountain King (Edvard Grieg) (6:35)

Personnel

Jeff Lynne – vocals, guitars, production
Bev Bevan – drums, percussion
Richard Tandy – piano, Moog, clavinet, Wurlitzer electric piano
Mike de Albuquerque – bass, backing vocals
Mike Edwards – cello
Mik Kaminski – violin (on tracks 1–4)
Ted Blight – cello (credited on the UK pressing, but said to be a figment of Lynne's imagination)
Wilf Gibson – violin (on tracks 5–9)
Colin Walker – cello (on tracks 5–9)
Marc Bolan – co-lead guitar (tracks 7 and 8)

Eldorado (1974)

All tracks written by Jeff Lynne

Side One

1. Eldorado Overture (2:12)
2. Can't Get It Out Of My Head (4:21)
3. Boy Blue (5:18)
4. Laredo Tornado (5:29)
5. Poor Boy (The Greenwood) (2:57)

Side Two

6. Mister Kingdom (5:50)
7. Nobody's Child (3:40)
8. Illusions In G Major (2:36)
9. Eldorado (5:20)
10. Eldorado Finale (1:20)

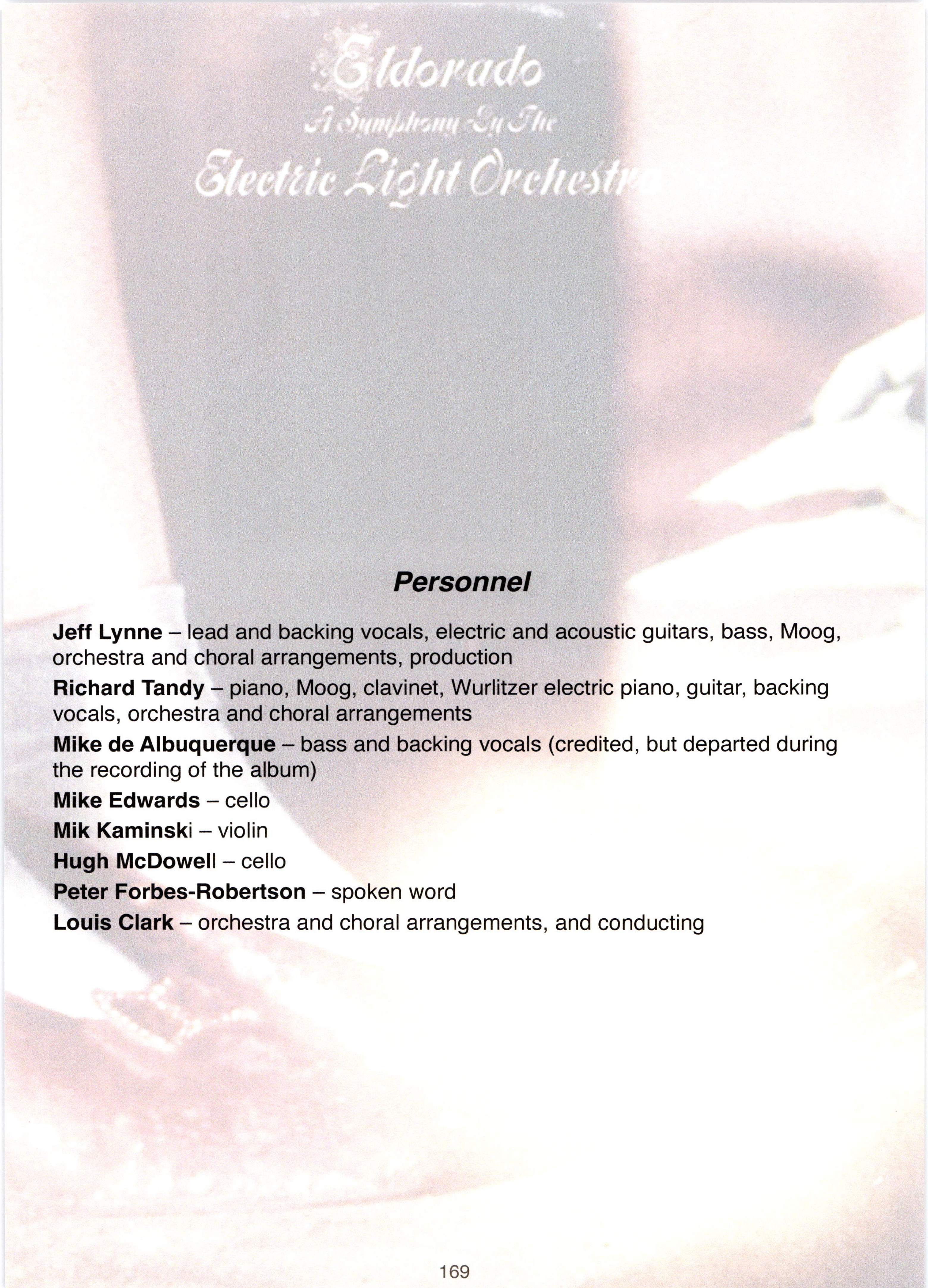

Personnel

Jeff Lynne – lead and backing vocals, electric and acoustic guitars, bass, Moog, orchestra and choral arrangements, production

Richard Tandy – piano, Moog, clavinet, Wurlitzer electric piano, guitar, backing vocals, orchestra and choral arrangements

Mike de Albuquerque – bass and backing vocals (credited, but departed during the recording of the album)

Mike Edwards – cello

Mik Kaminski – violin

Hugh McDowell – cello

Peter Forbes-Robertson – spoken word

Louis Clark – orchestra and choral arrangements, and conducting

Face The Music (1975)

All tracks written by Jeff Lynne

Side One
1. Fire On High (5:30)
2. Waterfall (4:11)
3. Evil Woman (4:35)
4. Nightrider (4:26)

Side Two
5. Poker (3:31)
6. Strange Magic (4:29)
7. Down Home Town (3:53)
8. One Summer Dream (5:47)

Personnel

Jeff Lynne – lead vocals, guitars, orchestral and choral arrangements, production
Bev Bevan – drums, percussion, spoken intro (backwards), backing vocals
Richard Tandy – piano, clavinet, Moog, guitar, Wurlitzer electric piano, tack piano, orchestral and choral arrangements
Kelly Groucutt – vocals, bass, backing vocals, lead vocals on track 5, co-lead vocals on track 4
Mik Kaminski – violin
Hugh McDowell – cello
Melvyn Gale – cello
Reinhold Mack – engineer
Louis Clark – orchestral and choral arrangements, and conducting
Ellie Greenwich – uncredited vocals
Susan Collins – uncredited vocals
Nancy O'Neill – uncredited vocals
Margaret Raymond – uncredited vocals
(Although Greenwich, Collins, O'Neill and Raymond are not credited as vocalists, the liner notes indicated "special thanks" to them.)

A New World Record (1976)

All tracks written by Jeff Lynne

Side One

1. Tightrope (5:00)
2. Telephone Line (4:38)
3. Rockaria! (3:12)
4. Mission (A World Record) (4:24)

Side Two

5. So Fine (3:55)
6. Livin' Thing (3:31)
7. Above The Clouds (2:16)
8. Do Ya (3:45)
9. Shangri-La (5:34)

Personnel

Jeff Lynne – lead vocals, electric and acoustic guitars, percussion, Wurlitzer 200 electric piano, orchestral and choral arrangements, production

Bev Bevan – drums, percussion, Minimoog "drum", backing vocals

Richard Tandy – Wurlitzer 200 electric piano, Minimoog, Micromoog, clavinet, piano, SLM Concert Spectrum, Mellotron M400, electric guitar, percussion, backing vocals, orchestral and choral arrangements

Kelly Groucutt – bass guitar, percussion, backing vocals, lead vocals

Mik Kaminski – violin

Hugh McDowell – cello, percussion

Melvyn Gale – cello

Mary Thomas – operatic vocals

Patti Quatro – uncredited backing vocals

Brie Brandt – uncredited backing vocals

Addie Lee – uncredited backing vocals

Reinhold Mack – engineer

Louis Clark – orchestral and choral arrangements, and conducting

Duane Scott – Engineer for USA edit

Out Of The Blue (1977)

All tracks written by Jeff Lynne

Side One
1. Turn To Stone (3:47)
2. It's Over (4:08)
3. Sweet Talkin' Woman (3:47)
4. Across The Border (3:52)

Side Two
5. Night In The City (4:02)
6. Starlight (4:30)
7. Jungle (3:51)
8. Believe Me Now (1:21)
9. Steppin' Out (4:38)

Side Three *(Concerto For A Rainy Day)*
1. Standin' In The Rain (4:20)
2. Big Wheels (5:10)
3. Summer And Lightning (4:13)
4. Mr. Blue Sky (5:05)

Side Four
5. Sweet Is The Night (3:26)
6. The Whale (5:05)
7. Birmingham Blues (4:21)
8. Wild West Hero (4:40)

Personnel

Jeff Lynne – lead and backing vocals, lead, rhythm and slide guitars (Gibson EDS-1275, Gibson Les Paul Custom, Gibson Marauder, Ovation 1615/4, Ovation 1619/4), Wurlitzer electric piano, Minimoog, orchestral and choral arrangements, production

Bev Bevan – Slingerland drums, Remo Rototoms, Avedis Zildjian cymbals, Slingerland Bev Bevan drumsticks, Remo drumheads, gong, various percussion instruments, backing vocals, fire extinguisher on 'Mr. Blue Sky'

Richard Tandy – Yamaha C7B piano, Yamaha CS-80, Wurlitzer electric piano, ARP 2600, Minimoog, Polymoog, ARP Omni, ARP Odyssey, Hohner clavinet, SLM Concert Spectrum, Mellotron M400, sequencers, Gibson SG Custom electric guitar, orchestral and choral arrangements

Kelly Groucutt – co-lead vocals on 'Sweet Is The Night', harmony and backing vocals, Gibson G3 bass guitar, percussion

Mik Kaminski – violin

Hugh McDowell – cello

Melvyn Gale – cello, jangle piano on 'Wild West Hero' (uncredited)

Shusei Nagaoka – artwork

Reinhold Mack – engineer

Louis Clark – orchestral and choral arrangements, and conducting

Stan Ricker (USA) and Kevin Metcalfe (UK) – original LP mastering

Discovery (1979)

All tracks written by Jeff Lynne

Side One
1. Shine A Little Love (4:43)
2. Confusion (3:42)
3. Need Her Love (5:11)
4. The Diary Of Horace Wimp (4:17)

Side Two
5. Last Train To London (4:32)
6. Midnight Blue (4:19)
7. On The Run (3:55)
8. Wishing (4:13)
9. Don't Bring Me Down (4:02)

Personnel

Jeff Lynne – lead vocals, guitars (electric, acoustic 12-string), vocoder, backing vocals, orchestral and choral arrangements, production

Bev Bevan – drums, percussion, backing vocals

Richard Tandy – piano, synthesiser, Wurlitzer electric piano, clavinet, lead guitar (track 6), backing vocals, orchestral and choral arrangements

Kelly Groucutt – bass guitar, backing vocals, lead vocals

Louis Clark - orchestral and choral arrangements, and conducting

Reinhold Mack – engineer

Mik Kaminski – violin (on the music videos)

Hugh McDowell – cello (on the music videos)

Melvyn Gale – cello (on the music videos)

Xanadu (1980)

Side One *(all tracks written by John Farrar)*
1. Magic (performed by Olivia Newton-John) (4:31)
2. Suddenly (performed by Olivia Newton-John with Cliff Richard) (4:02)
3. Dancin' (performed by Olivia Newton-John with The Tubes) (5:17)
4. Suspended In Time (performed by Olivia Newton-John) (3:55)
5. Whenever You're Away From Me (performed by Olivia Newton-John with Gene Kelly) (4:22)

Side Two *(all tracks written by Jeff Lynne)*
6. I'm Alive (performed by ELO) (3:46)
7. The Fall (performed by ELO) (3:34)
8. Don't Walk Away (performed by ELO) (4:48)
9. All Over The World (performed by ELO) (4:04)
10. Xanadu (performed by Olivia Newton-John and ELO) (3:28)

Side One Personnel

Olivia Newton-John – lead vocals, backing vocals
John Farrar – electric guitars, synthesisers, backing vocals
David Hungate – bass guitar on track 1 and track 4
David McDaniel – bass guitar on track 2
Ed Greene – drums, percussion (except on track 1)
Carlos Vega – drums, percussion on track 1
Jai Winding – electric piano on track 2
Michael Boddicker – vocoder on track 2
Cliff Richard – co-lead vocals on track 2
Fee Waybill – co-lead vocals on track 3
Roger Steen – guitars on track 3
Bill Spooner – guitars on track 3
Michael Cotten – synthesiser on track 3
Gene Kelly – co-lead vocals on track 5
Lou Halmy – whistling on track 5
Strings arranged and conducted by Richard Hewson
David J. Holman – engineer and mixer
Recorded and mixed at David J. Holman Studio in Laurel Canyon

Side Two Personnel

Jeff Lynne – lead vocals (except on track 10), backing vocals, electric guitars, acoustic guitars, keyboards, synthesisers
Bev Bevan – drums, percussion, tympani
Richard Tandy – pianos, synthesisers, keyboards
Kelly Groucutt – bass guitar, backing vocals
Olivia Newton-John – lead vocals on track 10
James Newton-Howard - synthesisers on track 10
Louis Clark - strings
Reinhold Mack – engineer
Recorded and mixed at Musicland Studios in Munich, Germany

Time (1981)

All tracks written by Jeff Lynne

Side One

1. Prologue (1:15)
2. Twilight (3:35)
3. Yours Truly, 2095 (3:15)
4. Ticket To The Moon (4:06)
5. The Way Life's Meant To Be (4:36)
6. Another Heart Breaks (3:46)

Side Two

7. Rain Is Falling (3:54)
8. From The End Of The World (3:16)
9. The Lights Go Down (3:31)
10. Here Is The News (3:49)
11. 21st Century Man (4:00)
12. Hold On Tight (3:05)
13. Epilogue (1:30)

Personnel

Jeff Lynne – lead and backing vocals, electric and acoustic guitars, piano, synthesisers, vocoder, production

Bev Bevan – drums, percussion

Richard Tandy – acoustic and electric pianos, synthesisers, vocoder, guitars

Kelly Groucutt – bass guitar, backing vocals

Bill Bottrell – engineer

Reinhold Mack – engineer

Rainer Pietsch – string conductor

Secret Messages (1983)

All tracks written by Jeff Lynne

Side One
1. Secret Messages (4:44)
2. Loser Gone Wild (5:27)
3. Bluebird (4:13)
4. Take Me On And On (4:57)

Side Two
5. Four Little Diamonds (4:05)
6. Stranger (4:27)
7. Danger Ahead (3:52)
8. Letter From Spain (2:51)
9. Train Of Gold (4:20)
10. Rock 'n' Roll Is King (3:49)

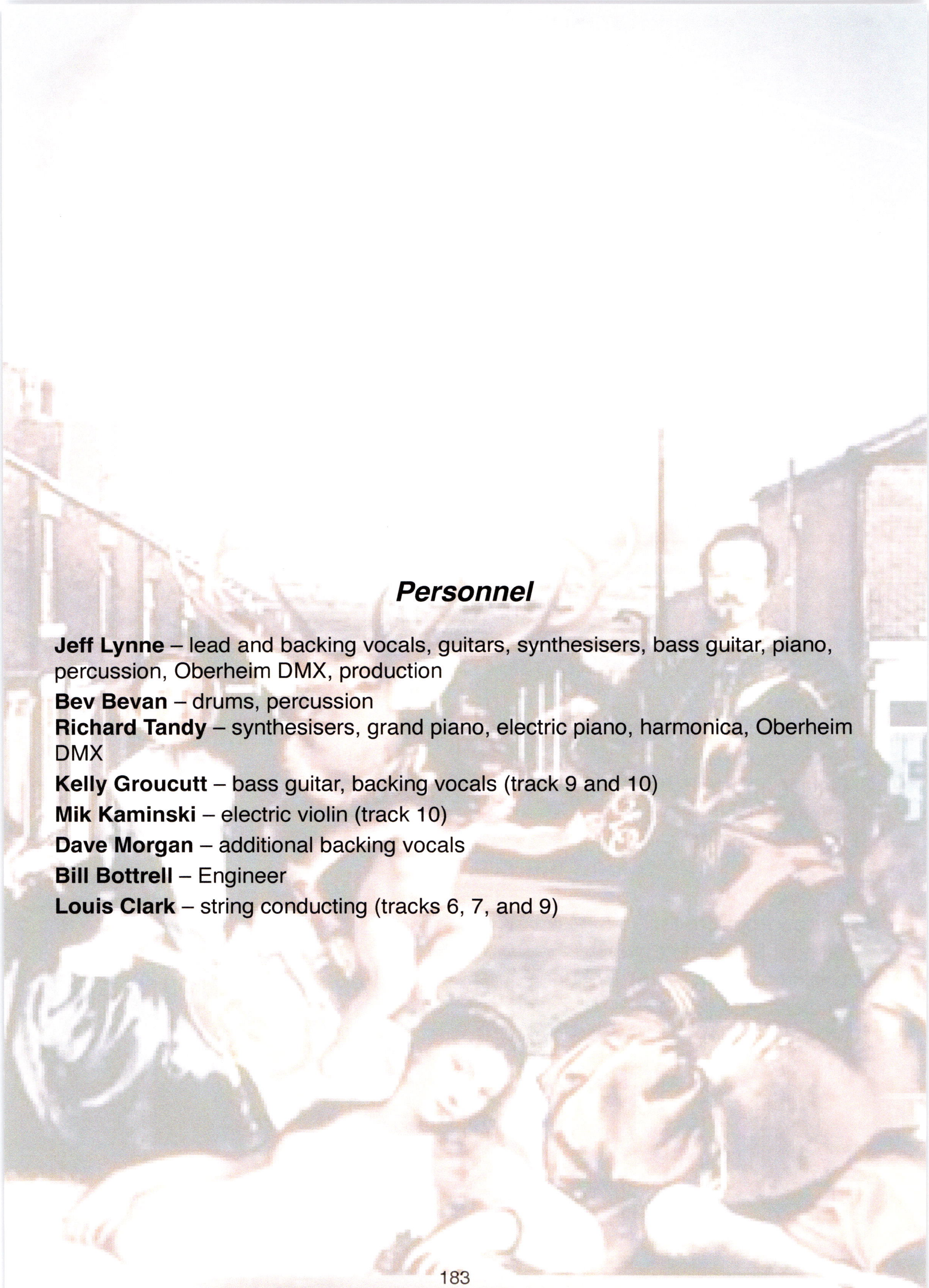

Personnel

Jeff Lynne – lead and backing vocals, guitars, synthesisers, bass guitar, piano, percussion, Oberheim DMX, production

Bev Bevan – drums, percussion

Richard Tandy – synthesisers, grand piano, electric piano, harmonica, Oberheim DMX

Kelly Groucutt – bass guitar, backing vocals (track 9 and 10)

Mik Kaminski – electric violin (track 10)

Dave Morgan – additional backing vocals

Bill Bottrell – Engineer

Louis Clark – string conducting (tracks 6, 7, and 9)

Balance Of Power (1986)

All tracks written by Jeff Lynne

Side One

1. Heaven Only Knows (2:52)
2. So Serious (2:38)
3. Getting To The Point (4:28)
4. Secret Lives (3:26)
5. Is It Alright (3:25)

Side Two

6. Sorrow About To Fall (3:59)
7. Without Someone (3:48)
8. Calling America (3:26)
9. Endless Lies (2:55)
10. Send It (3:04)

Personnel

Jeff Lynne – vocals, electric and acoustic guitars, Synclavier II computer synthesiser, bass guitar, keyboards, percussion, production

Bev Bevan – drums, percussion, drum programming

Richard Tandy – keyboards, sequence programming

Christian Schneider – saxophone

Bill Bottrell – engineer

Reinhold Mack – engineer

Zoom (2001)

All tracks written by Jeff Lynne

1. Alright (3:13)
2. Moment In Paradise (3:36)
3. State Of Mind (3:04)
4. Just For Love (3:40)
5. Stranger On A Quiet Street (3:41)
6. In My Own Time (3:03)
7. Easy Money (2:50)
8. It Really Doesn't Matter (3:20)
9. Ordinary Dream (3:23)
10. A Long Time Gone (3:15)
11. Melting In The Sun (3:10)
12. All She Wanted (3:14)
13. Lonesome Lullaby (4:02)

Personnel

Jeff Lynne – vocals, electric guitars, bass, keyboards, cello on track 11, drums, production

Richard Tandy – keyboards on track 2

George Harrison – slide guitar on tracks 10 and 12

Ringo Starr – drums on tracks 2 and 7

Marc Mann – rhythm guitar on track 2, string arrangements on tracks 6 and 11

Suzie Katayama – cello on tracks 4, 5, and 12

Roger Lebow – cello on track 13

Dave Boruff – saxophone on track 10

Laura Lynne – backing vocals on track 12

Rosie Vela – backing vocals on tracks 1 and 12, spoken parts and tap dancing on track 6

Kris Wilkinson – string arrangements on track 9

Alone In The Universe (2015)

All tracks written by Jeff Lynne

1. When I Was A Boy (3:12)
2. Love And Rain (3:29)
3. Dirty To The Bone (3:06)
4. When The Night Comes (3:22)
5. The Sun Will Shine On You (3:29)
6. Ain't It A Drag (2:34)
7. All My Life (2:50)
8. I'm Leaving You (3:07)
9. One Step At A Time (3:21)
10. Alone In The Universe (3:54)

Personnel

Jeff Lynne – lead and backing vocals, guitar, bass, piano, drums, keyboards, vibraphones, production, mixing

Steve Jay – shaker, tambourine, engineering, mixing

Laura Lynne – backing vocals on tracks 2 and 9

Craig Fruin – management

Bob Ludwig – mastering

Ryan Corey – design, illustration

Rob Shanahan – photography

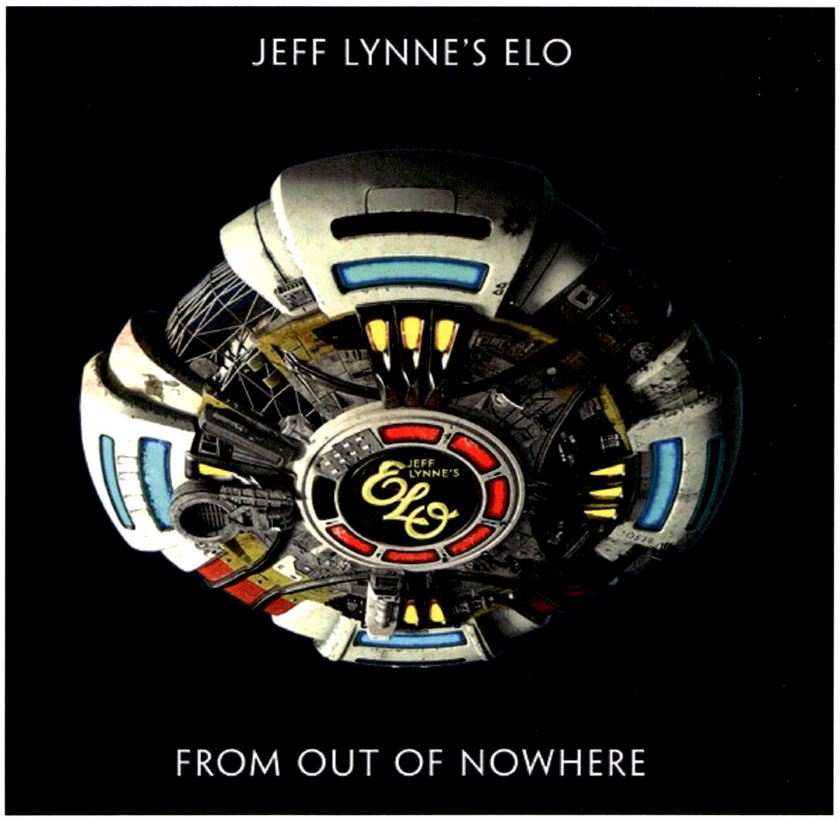

From Out Of Nowhere (2019)

All tracks written by Jeff Lynne

1. From Out Of Nowhere (3:14)
2. Help Yourself (3:14)
3. All My Love (3:06)
4. Down Came The Rain (3:29)
5. Losing You (3:36)
6. One More Time (3:28)
7. Sci-Fi Woman (3:07)
8. Goin' Out On Me (3:09)
9. Time Of Our Life (3:10)
10. Songbird (3:06)

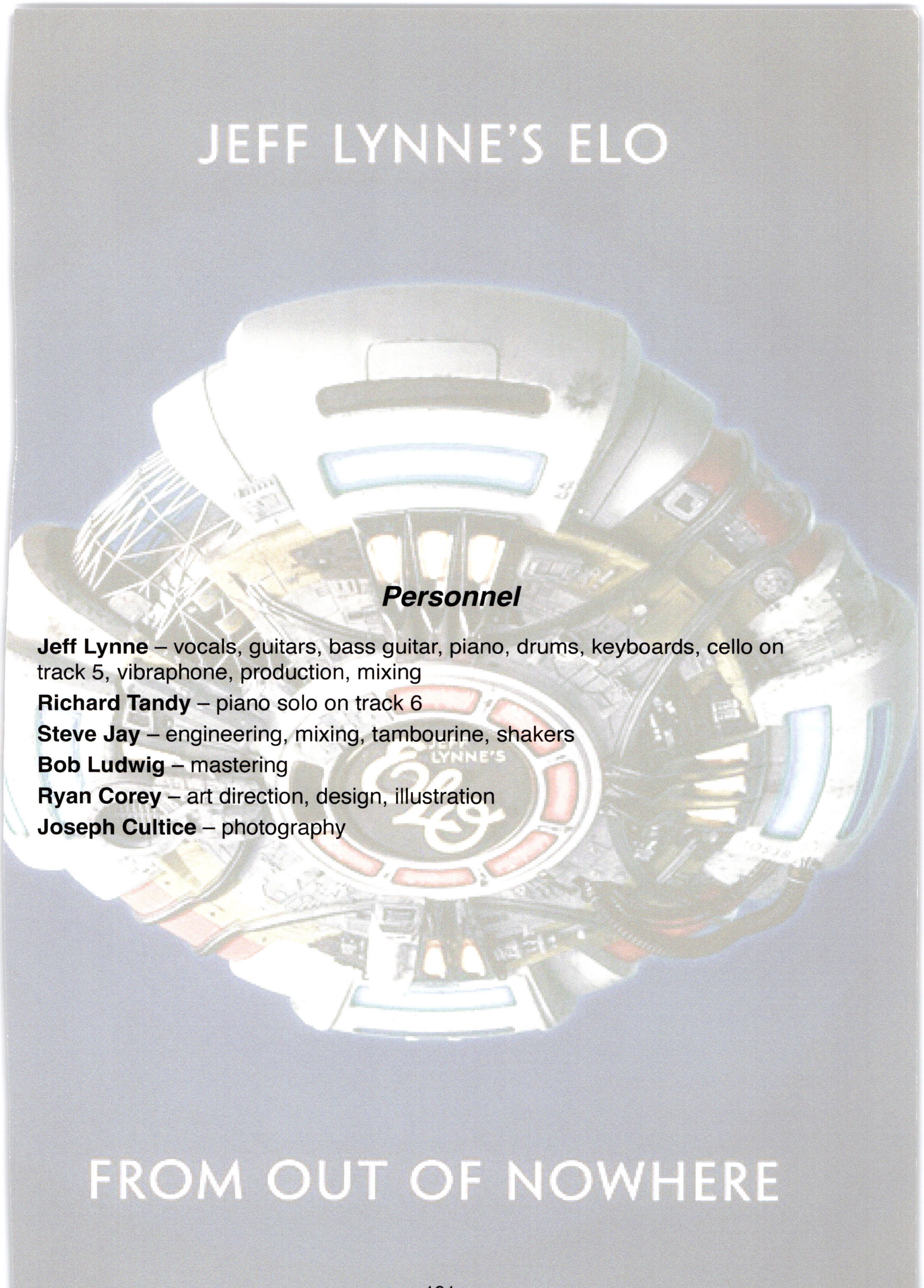

Personnel

Jeff Lynne – vocals, guitars, bass guitar, piano, drums, keyboards, cello on track 5, vibraphone, production, mixing
Richard Tandy – piano solo on track 6
Steve Jay – engineering, mixing, tambourine, shakers
Bob Ludwig – mastering
Ryan Corey – art direction, design, illustration
Joseph Cultice – photography

JEFF LYNNE'S
JEFF LYNNE'S
ELO
THE OVER AND OUT TOUR
AUG 24 PALM DESERT, CA
AUG 27 SEATTLE, WA
AUG 28 VANCOUVER, BC
AUG 30 PORTLAND, OR
SEP 01 SAN FRANCISCO, CA
SEP 06 SAINT LOUIS, MO
SEP 07 INDIANAPOLIS, IN
SEP 09 TORONTO, ON
SEP 10 PITTSBURGH, PA
SEP 13 CINCINNATI, OH
SEP 14 CLEVELAND, OH
SEP 16 NEW YORK, NY
SEP 20 PHILADELPHIA, PA
SEP 23 BOSTON, MA
SEP 25 WASHINGTON, DC
SEP 27 CHICAGO, IL
SEP 30 ST. PAUL, MN
OCT 02 DENVER, CO
OCT 09 DETROIT, MI
OCT 11 NASHVILLE, TN
OCT 12 ATLANTA, GA
OCT 15 AUSTIN, TX
OCT 16 HOUSTON, TX
OCT 18 DALLAS, TX
OCT 21 PHOENIX, AZ
OCT 23 SACRAMENTO, CA
OCT 25 INGLEWOOD, CA